# How to Dev

# Mindsets in t|

# The Complete Guide

# By Mike Gershon

## About the Author

Mike Gershon is known in the United Kingdom and beyond as an expert educationalist whose knowledge of teaching and learning is rooted in classroom practice. His online teaching tools have been viewed and downloaded more than 3.5 million times, making them some of the most popular of all time.

He is the author of over 80 books and guides covering different areas of teaching and learning. Some of Mike's bestsellers include books on assessment for learning, questioning, differentiation and outstanding teaching, as well as growth mindsets. You can train online with Mike, from anywhere in the world, at www.tes.com/institute/cpd-courses-teachers.

You can also find out more at www.mikegershon.com and www.gershongrowthmindsets.com, including about Mike's inspirational in-school training and student workshops.

## Training and Consultancy

Mike offers a range of training and consultancy services covering all areas of teaching and learning, raising achievement and classroom practice. Examples of recent training events include:

- Growth Mindsets: Staff Training, Student Workshops and Parent Workshop – Longton Primary School, Preston
- Assessment for Learning: Theory and Practice Keynote Address – Leigh Academies Trust Conference, London
- Effective Questioning to Raise Achievement – Shireland Collegiate Academy, Birmingham

To find out more, visit:

www.mikegershon.com

www.gershongrowthmindsets.com

Or get in touch via mike@mikegershon.com

## Other Works from the Same Author

**Available to buy now on Amazon:**

How to use Differentiation in the Classroom: The Complete Guide

How to use Assessment for Learning in the Classroom: The Complete Guide

How to use Bloom's Taxonomy in the Classroom: The Complete Guide

How to use Questioning in the Classroom: The Complete Guide

How to Develop Growth Mindsets in the Classroom: The Complete Guide

How to use Discussion in the Classroom: The Complete Guide

How to Manage Behaviour in the Classroom: The Complete Guide

How to Teach EAL Students in the Classroom: The Complete Guide

How to be an Outstanding Trainee Teacher: The Complete Guide

More Secondary Starters and Plenaries

Secondary Starters and Plenaries: History

Teach Now! History: Becoming a Great History Teacher

The Growth Mindset Pocketbook (with Professor Barry Hymer)

The Exams, Tests and Revision Pocketbook


**Also available to buy now on Amazon, the entire 'Quick 50' Series:**

50 Quick and Brilliant Teaching Ideas

50 Quick and Brilliant Teaching Techniques

50 Quick and Easy Lesson Activities

50 Quick Ways to Help Your Students Secure A and B Grades at GCSE

50 Quick Ways to Help Your Students Think, Learn, and Use Their Brains Brilliantly

50 Quick Ways to Motivate and Engage Your Students

50 Quick Ways to Outstanding Teaching

50 Quick Ways to Perfect Behaviour Management

50 Quick and Brilliant Teaching Games

50 Quick and Easy Ways Leaders Can Prepare for Ofsted

50 Quick and Easy Ways to Outstanding Group Work

50 Quick and Easy Ways to Prepare for Ofsted

50 Quick Ways to Stretch and Challenge More-Able Students

50 Quick Ways to Create Independent Learners

50 Quick Ways to go from Good to Outstanding

50 Quick Ways to Support Less-Able Learners


And forthcoming in Summer 2016:


50 Quick Ways to Get Past 'I Don't Know'

50 Quick Ways to Start Your Lesson with a Bang!

50 Quick Ways to Improve Literacy Across the Curriculum

50 Quick Ways to Improve Feedback and Marking

## Series Introduction

The 'How to...' series developed out of Mike's desire to share great classroom practice with teachers around the world. He wanted to put together a collection of books which would help professionals no matter what age group or subject they were teaching.

Each volume focuses on a different element of classroom practice and each is overflowing with brilliant, practical strategies, techniques and activities – all of which are clearly explained and ready-to-use. In most cases, the ideas can be applied immediately, helping teachers not only to teach better but to save time as well.

All of the books have been designed to help teachers. Each one goes out of its way to make educators' lives easier and their lessons even more engaging, inspiring and successful then they already are.

In addition, the whole series is written from the perspective of a working teacher. It takes account of the realities of the classroom, blending theoretical insight with a consistently practical focus.

The 'How to...' series is great teaching made easy.

## Acknowledgements

My thanks to all the staff and students I have worked with past and present, particularly those at Pimlico Academy and King Edward VI School, Bury St Edmunds. Thanks also to the teachers and teaching assistants who have attended my training sessions and who always offer great insights into what works in the classroom. Finally, thanks to Gordon at Kall Kwik for his design work and to Barry Hymer for the inspirational training session which first sparked my interest in growth mindsets.

# Contents

# Chapter One – Fixed vs Growth

## The Aim of This Book

Growth Mindset theory has gained in popularity in recent years. The research has been around for some time, but, as teachers and educators have realised the potential for transforming how students think about themselves and their learning, so has the attractiveness of the ideas grown.

The aim of this book is very simple. To provide a wide range of practical strategies, activities and techniques you can use to develop growth mindsets in your classroom. While we will look at Carol Dweck's research in this introductory chapter, the remainder of the book will focus on pedagogy. The things you can do as a teacher to change how your students think about talent, ability and intelligence. One chapter is devoted to empowering parents but, that aside, the focus remains resolutely on teaching.

For me, this is important. Growth mindsets research gives us the evidence we need to judge that this is an idea worth pursuing. Growth mindsets theory provides us with a framework through which to think. But, and as we all know, teaching is a practical business. We need to be able to bridge the gap between research and classroom reality. We need to take the ideas put forward by Dweck and her colleagues and turn them into the habits and actions of day-to-day teaching.

Nine chapters lie in wait for you. One looks at supporting parents, as mentioned. Of the other eight, seven focus on different areas of teaching and learning. Areas through which you can promote growth mindsets. And the eighth provides 175 ready-made growth mindset-style questions; twenty-five per area.

In all, the book contains more than sixty strategies, activities and techniques you can use to develop growth mindsets. For this reason, I hope the book might become a reference aid for you, acting as a starting point in your growth mindset journey, as well as a place to return to when in need of inspiration or a new idea.

It should be noted that all of the ideas presented are suitable for use across the age ranges and the curriculum, albeit with some adaptation or modification being necessary in places. I have tried to provide a range of examples covering different age groups. However, if an idea is exemplified through only one age group, don't take this to mean that it is only appropriate for children of that age. You can take the idea and apply it in your own context – altering it as you see fit, based on your knowledge and understanding of the children you teach.

So let us now look briefly at the research behind growth mindsets, before linking this to classroom practice and then, finally, outlining the chapters to come.

**Carol Dweck's Research**

Carol Dweck is Professor of Psychology at Stanford University. Her research into motivation, personality and development led her to state and define the terms growth mindset and fixed mindset. Through her work she has developed the theory that individuals possess implicit theories of intelligence, with these sitting on a continuum running from growth mindset at one end to fixed mindset at the other.

Dweck's work suggests that those individuals currently operating from a fixed mindset believe that success is a result of innate factors, whereas those thinking through a growth mindset see it as a result of hard work, persistence, training and learning.

There are two key books written by Dweck which explore and explain her research. The first is an academic text called 'Self-Theories: Their Role in Motivation, Personality and Development'. The second is a book aimed at a mainstream audience, called 'Mindset: How You Can Fulfil Your Potential'. I would recommend reading both. They provide excellent foundations for making changes to your teaching.

Lots of material is also available online, including video footage as well as text. Here is a collection of links for you to explore:

- **mindsetonline.com/abouttheauthor/** - a biography of Dweck, a homepage for her book, and links to various articles.

- **teacherstoolbox.co.uk/T_Dweck.html** - Geoff Petty explains Dweck's theory of motivation and looks at the implications for teachers.
- **www.ted.com/talks/** - here you can find a 10-minute TED talk by Dweck.
- **psychology.stanford.edu/cdweck** - Dweck's Stanford homepage, including lots of papers in PDF form you can download and read.
- **alumni.stanford.edu/get/page/magazine/article/?article_id=32124** – an article looking at effort and Dweck's research.
- **nymag.com/news/features/27840/** - an article about the inverse power of praise.
- **www.scientificamerican.com/article/the-secret-to-raising-smart-kids1/** - an article by Dweck about parenting.
- **www.edweek.org/ew/articles/2015/09/23/carol-dweck-revisits-the-growth-mindset.html** - an article by Dweck looking at how some of her growth mindset work has been misapplied in the classroom – and how to avoid this.
- **www.youtube.com/watch?v=QGvR_0mNpWM** - a 26-minute video of Dweck presenting growth mindset ideas.
- **www.youtube.com/watch?v=hiiEeMN7vbQ** - a 9-minute video of Dweck: 'Developing a Growth Mindset'.
- **www.youcubed.org/** - a Stanford maths learning website heavily influenced by growth mindsets research.

In 'Self-Theories', Dweck details a large number of experiments she and her colleagues conducted, looking at how students perceive themselves, their learning and what it is possible to achieve. She focuses on the idea that we possess theories of intelligence. That is, theories about what intelligence is, how it manifests and, therefore, how it can or can't be changed.

Two theories of intelligence are identified: entity theory and incremental theory.

The first accords with a fixed mindset perspective. The second accords with a growth mindset perspective.

Put simply, an entity theory of intelligence means you believe intelligence is a finite entity. Something you and everyone else possesses and which is fixed and unchanging, differing from person to person. An incremental theory of intelligence means you believe intelligence is open to change – that it can grow incrementally depending on the actions you take. And that this is true of everybody.

Dweck notes in her research that the theory of intelligence under which a student operates has significant consequences. It influences – possibly even determines – how they are likely to respond in certain situations, what they are likely to see as being possible, how they think about themselves, and the extent to which they enjoy learning and being challenged.

With this in mind, let us build out of Dweck's research and clarify precisely what we mean when we talk about growth mindsets.

**What are Growth Mindsets?**

Mindsets are beliefs; the set of beliefs we hold about ourselves and what it is possible for us to do. These beliefs underpin and influence our thinking which, in turn, gives rise to actions. When it comes to learning, students may have a growth mindset, a fixed mindset, or a mixture of the two. In the latter case, this might see them having a growth mindset in certain subjects and a fixed mindset in others.

It is important to remember that mindsets are open to change. They are just thoughts, after all. So, for example, a student who currently has a fixed mindset towards maths need not have this mindset in the future. Similarly, and less happily, a student with a growth mindset towards English may lose this if they suffer a bad transition from primary to secondary school.

Fixed and growth mindsets begin from a central premise. This is the central belief on which they rest. Conclusions are derived from this starting point. To put it another way, a series of further beliefs flow from the first belief.

The central premise of a fixed mindset is that intelligence, ability and talent are fixed and static. This is the entity theory of intelligence.

The central premise of a growth mindset is that intelligence, ability and talent can go up or down. This is the incremental theory of intelligence.

The following beliefs tend to follow on from the fixed mindset premise: effort is pointless; feedback should be avoided; so too challenges; it doesn't make sense to persist at something if you can't already do it; there's little point in thinking about your own thinking.

Notice how each of these beliefs follows logically from the central premise. If you believe that talent, intelligence and ability are fixed, then it makes sense to see effort as pointless. This is a logical conclusion of the central premise. Similarly, if you believe you cannot change, then why would you bother with feedback? This won't have any impact as what you have is what you have, regardless of what anybody else tells you to do.

The following beliefs tend to follow on from the growth mindset premise: effort is the path to mastery; feedback can help you to develop and grow; challenges are learning opportunities and can be embraced; persisting at something helps you to get better at it; thinking about your own thinking means finding ways to improve it.

Again, the beliefs follow logically from the central premise. If you believe that talent, intelligence and ability can go up or down, then it makes sense to see effort as a path to mastery. Similarly, it is logical to acknowledge that persistence can help you to get better at something. The act of persisting allows you to practice, observe what works and what doesn't, learn from your mistakes and, as a result of all this, get better at the thing in question.

This leads to two conclusions. First, when we are seeking to promote growth mindsets in the classroom we are seeking to promote to every student the central premise that talent, intelligence and ability can go up or down. Second, to do this we can focus on both this central premise and on the different conclusions which flow from it.

**The Habits of a Growth Mindset**

Students with a growth mindset begin with the belief that intelligence, talent and ability can go up or down. This tends to lead to some or all of the following habits:

- Effort is seen as a path to mastery. Students believe that by applying effort – and targeting it effectively – you can learn, develop and grow.
- Challenge is seen as something useful and is often embraced. Students understand that challenges push us to do more than we can currently manage. They appreciate that you can learn from challenges and that, over time, the challenge will become manageable and then easy.
- Mistakes are not necessarily loved but they are seen as something from which you can learn. This is accompanied by the belief that failure is not the be all and end all. Instead, we can learn from failure, picking ourselves up and trying again.
- Feedback gives you information you can use to improve or develop your work. This does not mean that feedback is always received with relish, but it does mean that students are able to put emotional reactions to one side and make use of the feedback by applying it to their learning.
- Thinking is seen as open to change. As part of this, students see the benefit of thinking about their own thinking (metacognition). They understand that by attending to your thoughts you can identify what is working and what isn't, before using this to make changes, refinements and improvements.
- Persistence in the face of obstacles is a good thing. Students are more likely to persist when faced with obstacles. Their thinking is animated by the belief that effort leads to mastery and that you are in a position to alter what you can currently do. Therefore, persevering has benefits (and is likely to lead to good outcomes).
- Students are more likely to have a go at things and not fear the consequences of being wrong. They understand that we learn through trial and error. And they appreciate that you can't develop and grow unless you try new things.

When promoting growth mindsets in our classrooms it is these habits we seek to cultivate. By doing this we help students to become more resilient. The process sees us developing their character as well as their knowledge and understanding.

**Fixed Vs. Growth**

Cognitive psychology focuses on our thinking. It does not deny the impact of biological and genetic factors, but it does focus on cognition – how we think – as opposed to the influence of genes and biology. Cognitive psychologists suggest that our thinking has a significant impact on our behaviour. How we think influences what we do, the decisions we make and the consequences which follow.

When it comes to learning, the argument we can take from Dweck's research is that the mindset a student possesses underpins their thinking. For example, if a student believes that they simply can't do maths and that no amount of effort, persistence or perseverance will change this then certain behaviours, decisions and consequences are likely to follow. On the other hand, if a student believes that you can get better at maths and that effort, persistence and perseverance have an important role to play, then different behaviours, decisions and consequences will follow.

This illustrates the extent to which fixed mindsets and growth mindsets are representative of two different ways of thinking about learning and your own potential for change. Students operating under a fixed mindset set an arbitrary limit on what they believe they are capable of achieving. Students operating under a growth mindset set no such limit. This doesn't mean that these students believe they can achieve anything and everything. But it does mean they don't circumscribe their ability to act – and to benefit from the cumulative gains which stem from consistently acting in a positive and determined manner.

One way of cultivating growth mindsets is to think of it as akin to promoting a change in how your class, school, or individual students think about learning. This also indicates how effective embedding of growth mindsets takes time. This is an intervention which is as much about forming new habits as it is anything else.

Those habits are habits of thought. Some of them are general, such as the habit of thinking that your abilities are open to change. Some of them are specific, such as the habit of persisting even if the work feels difficult. And some of them are about dealing with emotions, such as learning to separate emotional reactions from rational decision-making. To illustrate the last point, consider how a student can learn to put the disappointment of failure to one side so that they can instead focus on using the information failure reveals. This habit of thought allows a student to learn from failure even if there is an emotional reaction attached to it.

### Common Growth Mindset Myths

Growth mindsets are not a panacea. Dweck's research simply offers us a powerful lens through which to look at student thinking and learning, and to then try to effect change. The tenets of growth mindset thinking – seeing effort as a path to mastery, learning from mistakes, embracing challenge, using feedback, thinking about your own thinking – chime with much of what we would see as good classroom practice. Taking a growth mindset approach when teaching often means giving these things a bigger role, at the same time as we draw students' attention to how they are thinking about themselves and their abilities and, where appropriate, offer them an alternative story to tell.

As with any popular classroom approach, myths have developed. Here are five of the most common, along with a rebuttal.

- **Myth: Growth Mindsets just means saying 'yet'.** Using 'yet', as in: 'you can't do it yet…' is one technique among many. It does not constitute change on its own, but is a useful starting point for altering the language of your classroom. We will look at this in more detail in Chapter Two.
- **Myth: Growth Mindsets implies that everyone can be super successful at anything.** This is not the case. Growth mindsets makes a much weaker claim, but one which is far easier to defend. It suggests that all students can learn, therefore changing their intelligence, talent and ability and that this is more likely to occur if students begin from a premise that their talent, ability and intelligence is open to change.
- **Myth: Growth Mindsets just means praising effort regardless.** This is not true. Instead, growth mindsets means promoting the

idea that effort is a path to mastery. However, we are talking about targeted effort. That is, effort which has purpose and direction. Praising effort regardless is something different entirely. We will look at this in detail in Chapter Four.

- **Myth: Growth Mindsets ignores biological factors.** Growth mindsets focuses on cognition – the thinking students do. It does not examine biological influences because it comes from the cognitive school of psychology. However, this does not mean it denies the influence of biological factors.
- **Myth: Growth Mindsets means labelling students as having a fixed or growth mindset.** The central premise of growth mindsets is that we are all open to change. Therefore, labelling is not to be welcomed as it presupposes a fixed state over which the individual has no control. Students have mindsets, these are open to change. The likelihood is that they will have different mindsets in different areas of their life, leading to a mixture of fixed and growth. A teacher's goal is to promote growth mindsets and the tenets which constitute this so as to help all students gain a sense of agency over their learning.

**Performance Goals and Learning Goals**

Here is a quote from 'Self-Theories':

"A performance goal is about measuring ability. It focuses students on measuring themselves from their performance, and so when they do poorly they may condemn their intelligence and fall into a helpless response.

A learning goal is about mastering new things. The attention here is on finding strategies for learning. When things don't go well, this has nothing to do with the student's intellect. It simply means that the right strategies have not yet been found. Keep looking." (Dweck: 2000, page 16)

Performance goals create a zero-sum game. The student has a bar they must meet. They either meet it, or they don't. If they don't, and as the quote implies, they may respond by assuming there is something wrong with them.

Learning goals are never a zero-sum game. They are an ongoing, continuous process. For this reason, they reflect the reality of life much more accurately than performance goals.

An excessive focus on performance goals is likely to promote an entity theory of intelligence and to encourage fixed mindset thinking from students. It may also cause students to fall into a trap of helplessness. On failing to reach a performance goal they tell themselves that they don't have what is necessary to be successful. Therefore, what can they possibly do to meet the standards they have been set?

Promoting learning goals means getting students to focus on the process of learning and to think about what is required to master new things. This involves persistence, trying out different strategies, repetition, making mistakes and learning from trial and error. Talking in terms of learning goals means sending students the message that everybody's intelligence is open to change, and that this change is a direct function of the different things you choose to do.

This leads us to an important point sitting just beneath the surface of growth mindset theory.

An incremental view of intelligence – a growth mindset perspective – gives students a much greater degree of agency than an entity view – a fixed mindset perspective.

This agency stems from the fact that the student believes their efforts can effect change. Note how this compares with the idea of helplessness mentioned in the quote and connected to performance goals.

It is worth remembering this point as you seek to develop growth mindsets in your classroom. The process in which you are engaged is in part about giving students agency. Helping them to take control of their learning. Helping them to understand that they have the power to act in ways that lead to learning, development and the achievement of goals.

This is education for life, as well as the classroom.

## Mindset Theory and the Classroom: Changing How Students Think

How, then, do we go about developing growth mindsets in the classroom? What is it that we are trying to do when we say that we want to make growth mindsets a reality for our students?

Above all else, it comes down to changing how students think.

As we have seen, mindsets are sets of beliefs. Beliefs give rise to actions. The hope is that by changing some of these beliefs, different actions will follow.

If students are operating from a fixed mindset perspective, if they are working under the auspices of an entity theory of intelligence, then we want to try to change this. We want to help them see themselves differently. To see learning in a different light.

Our aim is to teach in such a way that we give students every opportunity to change how they think. To adjust the set of beliefs they take as their starting point. We are looking to help them establish new habits of thought. Habits which make it easier for them to achieve more. That help them to enjoy learning more. And that give them greater resolve and an enhanced sense of agency.

What we need to do, then, is translate growth mindset theory into a set of areas on which we can focus our attention while we are planning, teaching and assessing. These areas will tally with different elements of growth mindset thinking, and give us ample opportunity to offer students alternative ways to think and act.

We are looking for a set of practical categories which accord with growth mindset theory and which also offer scope for a variety of teaching and learning interventions. After all, you need to make mindsets your own. You need strategies, activities and techniques which suit your style of teaching and the students with whom you work.

Identifying these areas is the first step. Presenting a range of practical measures is the second step. This we will do in Chapters Two to Nine. The third step is selecting the techniques that feel right for you, trialling these, adapting them and then persisting with them. After all, it is through persistence that real change will come. Altering how students think takes time. As does forming new habits. Developing growth mindsets is an ongoing process. A learning goal, rather than a performance one.

**Classroom Practice and the Chapters Which Follow**

Here then, are the practical areas we will look at. Each is briefly explained, with a summary of what you can expect to find in the pages which follow.

**Chapter Two: Getting the Language Right:** The language students use to talk about themselves and their learning reflects and reinforces how they think. In this chapter we look at ways in which you can give them different language with which to talk and think. This includes examining the stories students tell about themselves, and the alternative stories we can share with them.

**Chapter Three: Changing How Students Perceive Mistakes:** Mistakes are part of learning. If students fear them and seek to avoid them, then they will miss out on myriad opportunities to learn and develop. In this chapter we look at a host of ways through which you can change how students perceive mistakes. The aim is to give you a set of tools you can use to help students view mistakes in a positive light.

**Chapter Four:  Targeting Student Effort:** Effort matters. Effort is the path to mastery. But unfocussed or thoughtlessly applied effort does not have much of an impact. Effort needs to be targeted, and it needs to be targeted as effectively as possible. In this chapter we look at how to make effort the focus of your classroom, and how you can ensure students are targeting their efforts in productive ways, whenever and wherever possible.

**Chapter Five: Giving Great Feedback:** Students operating under a growth mindset are more likely to see feedback as helpful. Something to take on board and use in their efforts to achieve mastery. In this chapter we look at how to give feedback which encourages a growth mindset perspective and how to help students implement and see the benefits of any feedback they receive.

**Chapter Six: Thinking about Thinking:** If you think about your own thinking it means you are well placed to change that thinking. It also means you are more likely to perceive that thinking as being open to change. As something which is malleable and not fixed. In this chapter we look at what you can do to promote metacognition in your classroom, focussing on strategies you can employ to help all students see their thinking as being open to change.

**Chapter Seven: Creating a Challenge Culture:** Students operating under a growth mindset are more likely to embrace challenges. They are also more likely to see the benefits challenges bring in terms of learning, growth and development. Ideally, we want all students to embrace challenge, to see this as the norm and not to fear the problems and potential difficulties that challenge can bring. In this chapter we look at a range of ways through which you can make this happen.

**Chapter Eight: Focussing on Processes:** Processes are the things we do while we are learning, while we are thinking and in order to create products. Focussing on processes means helping students to think about learning goals instead of performance goals. It means giving them a chance to observe and analyse how what they do leads to specific results; and why it is in their power to change and develop their processes. In this chapter we look at techniques you can employ to bring processes to life and to help students think differently about their learning.

**Chapter Nine: Engaging Parents with Growth Mindsets:** Parents have a huge influence on their children. More than any teacher. More than the school as a whole. If students hear messages at home that clash with the growth mindset messages we communicate in the classroom, then changing how they think becomes more difficult. In this chapter we look at a variety of strategies you can use to engage parents with growth mindsets, as well as tools you can share so they can help their children at home.

**Chapter Ten: Growth Mindset Questions:** In our final chapter we present 175 growth mindset inspired questions. Ready for you to use as they are, or to adapt as you see fit. There are twenty-five questions for each of the areas outlined above (and a further twenty-five questions for parents within Chapter Nine). This gives a great starting point for developing growth mindsets through your interactions with students.

And with that we conclude our introduction. All that is left for me to say is read on and enjoy! I hope you find lots of strategies you can use in your day-to-day teaching. I'm sure your mission to develop growth mindsets in the classroom will be a great success. And, if at first you don't succeed, keep targeting your efforts until you do!

# Chapter Two – Getting the Language Right

## Introduction

Language reflects and shapes our thoughts. It gives us a means to articulate how we think and feel at the same time as it allows us to understand those thoughts and feelings. Yet, we can also be trapped by language, with the words we speak reinforcing a perception which might run counter to what we really want – or to the nature of things as they really are.

Attending to your language means viewing it critically at the same time as you use it instrumentally – as a tool through which to communicate and as a means by which to bridge the gap between minds.

In the classroom, the language we present to students is a model. It is imbued with authority and weight – both from the role we play as teacher and from our standing as an adult, an expert and an individual.

We must also remember that students are continually developing their language skills as they progress through school, from the very beginning to the very end. This development encompasses what they read and hear as well as what they say, write, and think.

When it comes to growth mindsets, language is where we must begin. The words we use in the classroom need to accord with the characteristics we are seeking to cultivate. It is no use telling students they shouldn't fear making mistakes in the same breath as you criticise them for getting things wrong.

Nor is it any use in assuring students that everybody's intelligence, talent and ability are open to change if you then remind them that you, just like them, do not have the maths gene, and so don't worry about it.

This last example illustrates how fixed mindset language can slip out even when our intentions are good. A statement such as this is predicated on a desire to empathise with the student in question. But this attempted empathy only serves to reinforce the idea that mathematical ability is innate. That you either have it or you don't.

So this chapter sets out with two aims. First, to present ways in which you can help students to change the language they use to talk about learning, thinking, themselves, and their own abilities. Second, to give you ways to keep an eye on your own language, through which to adapt and change it, and through which you can be sure you are promoting growth mindset characteristics whenever you are in the classroom.

As a final point, I would note that every other chapter in this book includes reference, either explicit or implicit, to language and its role in developing growth mindsets. This is inevitable. We cannot change how students view mistakes without talking about them. Nor can we give much useful feedback in non-linguistic form. This chapter, however, seeks to keep language front and centre. Something you might choose to do when first trying to cultivate growth mindset thinking through your teaching.

**Giving Students Growth Mindset Language**

Here are some words associated with growth mindsets:

- Effort
- Challenge
- Perseverance
- Thinking
- Learning
- Feedback
- Decisions
- Challenge
- Mistakes
- Good Mistakes
- Failure
- Useful Failure
- Trial and Error
- Trial and Improvement
- Thinking about Thinking
- Metacognition
- Reflection
- Persistence
- Process

- Grit
- Determination
- Growth
- Resilience
- Learning Goals
- Change
- Incremental

This is the starting point for helping students to talk and think about growth mindsets. Both in terms of knowing what a mindset is and also in the wider sense of knowing what characteristics will help them to learn, to overcome challenges and to enjoy both these things.

Introducing students to growth mindset vocabulary means giving them a new set of words to think with. It also provides them with a means to articulate the experiences they have in the classroom. Finally, it may be that these words stand as a counterpoint to the language some students already associate with learning and thinking.

When introducing this new vocabulary to students, decide in advance which words matter most to you, and which words you really want to have currency in your classroom. The above list is too long to be used all in one go. Students will be overloaded. Picking a choice selection of words or phrases is a great way to begin.

For example, some teachers I've worked with really like the idea of 'good mistakes' and 'trial and improvement'. For them, these phrases struck a chord. So they decided to kick off their growth mindsets journey by introducing these concepts to their students, and then returning to them again and again. Over time, the students came to use the phrases as well. They could spot a good mistake, talk about why it was a good mistake, and explain what you could learn from it.

An added benefit of choosing a set of words or phrases which work for you is that you will be more likely to persist in your use of them. Meaning gives us a sense of purpose. This, in turn, keeps motivation high. If you choose words arbitrarily, or have some foisted on you, then the likelihood of them still being in circulation six months later is much lower.

Finally, don't be afraid to play around with different ways to introduce your chosen words to students. Here are some examples of how to get started:

- Create a wall display based around the words.
- Get students to create work (posters, guides, leaflets) based on the words.
- Plan and teach an entire lesson based around the words or phrases. A lesson looking at good mistakes through history, alongside the role of trial and improvement in technological change, is a great way to get students inspired, engaged and used to using these new phrases.
- Engage students in call and response so they can practice saying the words. This works particularly well with younger children and also creates a sense of ownership over the words.
- Use the words as part of the feedback and praise your deliver, both written and verbal.
- Start a class game of 'spot the example'. Students are tasked with spotting examples of the chosen words or phrases in every lesson. One class might be asked to spot examples of determination they see in their own work, in other people's work, and outside their lessons.
- Model using the words in conversation – either with a student or with another teacher. Give students role-play scenarios through which they can practice using and thinking about the words. If appropriate, contrast these with opposite examples (determination vs giving up; trial and improvement vs try it once then stop).

**Growth Mindset Diamond 9**

Here's an example of a specific activity you can use to help your students think about, discuss and evaluate some of the different characteristics associated with growth and fixed mindsets. It gives them an opportunity to practice using the words, to manipulate them and to reflect on how they could influence their thinking.

Display a set of nine words or phrases on the board. For example:

- Effort
- Determination
- Using trial and error
- Getting feedback
- Guessing
- Not giving up
- Taking the easy option
- Copying others
- Thinking about your learning

Alongside this, show students an empty 'Diamond 9'. That is, a set of nine boxes arranged in a diamond shape. One at the top, followed by two, followed by three, then two and, finally, one at the bottom.

Indicate that the top box is the most important box and that the bottom box is the least important. Ask students to work in pairs to place the nine words or phrases into the nine boxes. Encourage them to discuss their choices and to make a note of their final decisions, along with their reasons why.

When sufficient time has passed, invite pairs to team up into groups of four. Give each pair two minutes to talk to their new partners about their decisions. Explain that they should try to convince them why their choices are right. After this, give groups time in which to see if they can agree a shared 'Diamond 9'.

Bring the class back together and lead a discussion in which different groups have a chance to share their thinking. Probe the comments students make. Encourage them to go into detail about their choices and to explain in full why they chose what they chose. Conclude the activity by asking if the class are prepared to come up with a whole-class 'Diamond 9'. If they are, lead them in this. If they are not, explain that as an alternative you would like them to agree on the three most important words or phrases, without putting these in a specific order.

What, then, does this activity do?

First, it give students a great opportunity to play around with a set of words and phrases. This helps them to think carefully about these, and to familiarise themselves with them. Second, it gives you an opportunity to circulate, listen to what students are saying and either store this information for future reference or use it as the basis of further questioning. Third, it ask students to reflect on what they imagine effective learning to involve. This can provide some revealing insights – and gives a great starting point from which to analyse what you need to do next to support all the pupils in your class in developing growth mindsets.

**Pay Attention to Stories – Yours and Theirs**

The stories we tell about ourselves often reinforce the perceptions we have about what is and what is not possible. Similarly, the stories other people tell about us can influence, even circumscribe, how we think and act.

Sometimes these stories manifest themselves within language, rather than being described by language. Here is an example to show the difference:

**Story described by language:** I'm not a maths person. Maths isn't me and it never has been.

**Story manifested in language:** I can't do it. Leave me alone. I don't want to try again.

In the first example, the story is narrated by the student. They are telling us – telling themselves – a story they may have told many times before. In the second example, the story lies beneath the language. It underpins the things the student is saying. We need to intuit this story, while accepting that what we derive may not be one hundred percent accurate. If I heard a student saying something like this, I might surmise that the story lying beneath is something akin to: 'I've made mistakes in the past and it hasn't turned out well. I don't want to make mistakes now because I don't want to go through that kind of thing all over again.'

This same point is true of the stories we might tell about students – sometimes wittingly, sometimes unwittingly. For example:

**Story described by language:** I remember last week when you kept going, even though things were really tough. That's the kind of learner you are. Someone who looks at problems and keeps trying to find solutions.

**Story manifested in language:** Art wasn't my thing, either. I can still remember how hard I found it. Sometimes you've just got to accept your limitations. Don't worry if you'll never be any good at it.

The first example shows how we can tell students growth mindset stories in which they are the subject, based on our perception of what we think is possible and what we want to encourage them to do. The second example illustrates the potential for slipping into fixed mindset language even with good intentions. Here, the underlying story is that people have fixed abilities when it comes to art, so don't worry. This reflects an entity view of intelligence, talent and ability that we want to avoid.

All of this leads us to a strong conclusion. We need to pay attention to the stories in our classrooms – ours and our students'. This means listening carefully to what we hear and, if necessary, reframing it back to students in a growth mindset style. Or offering an alternative story as a counterpoint.

It also means thinking about the content of our words before we speak, and catching ourselves if we spot an unintended slip into a fixed mindset story, however well-intentioned we may believe our actions may be.

### Growth Mindset Story-Telling

Stories have power, as we've just seen. They are one of the fundamental ways through which we make sense of the world. You could even argue that our mindset is a story we tell about ourselves – what we think is possible and what we think is beyond our reach. When we retell stories over and again they tend to become more deeply embedded in our sense of self.

Equally, if we constantly hear stories about ourselves from others, these can be taken on board as a statement of fact. Witness, for example, the child who has been told a hundred times that the Smith family do not have the maths gene and who, as a result, dutifully believes that they cannot do maths and will never be able to change their ability.

One way to counter fixed mindset stories, and to provide students with alternative stories they can tell about themselves, their abilities and their efforts, is to share fiction and non-fiction stories illustrating key growth mindset principles.

For younger students, fiction is often the best port of call. Whereas older students can find it easier to identify with real-life examples (though feel free to prove me wrong!).

When using growth mindset stories in your classroom, consider in advance how you will encourage students to discuss and think about the key messages. For example, you might plan a series of questions to provoke thinking about the nature of effort. Or, you might set students the challenge of writing their own story, based on the tenets of the story you shared.

There are plenty of fictional stories which embody growth mindset principles. Fables, myths and fairy-tales are a good place to start. Particularly Aesop's fables, with the moral dimension driving many toward an exposition of character which tallies well with growth mindset principles.

When it comes to non-fiction, case studies of individuals are good. Examples I have used include:

- Thomas Edison (trial and improvement)
- James Dyson (learning from mistakes)
- J.K. Rowling (persistence; putting failure – in the form of rejection – to one side)
- Paula Radcliffe (effort; determination)
- Michael Jordan (focus on processes; mistakes as a path to learning)

Many more are out there, and I'm sure you have your own favourites.

Another non-fiction storytelling device you can use is that of the former student. Here, we use stories about pupils we have taught to illustrate the way in which anybody can take growth mindset principles and make them their own. For example, we might tell our current students a story about a child who was predicted a D grade but came out with an A. Not because they focussed obsessively on the performance goal of getting an A, but because they refused to believe there was a limit to their potential, and so used effort, determination and feedback to develop their skills until such a time as they had mastered the subject.

This type of storytelling is even more powerful if you invite the student in question back to speak to your class.

**Reframing**

You may come across students using language which reflects the beliefs of a fixed mindset. For example:

- I can't do it
- I'll never be able to do it
- This isn't me
- I'm not an Art person
- There's no way I'll ever be able to get the hang of this

In each case, the student's words imply they have a fixed sum of intelligence which it is impossible to change. This entity theory of intelligence manifests itself through how they choose to talk about themselves.

When seeking to develop growth mindsets we want to shift student language away from this. However, simply telling students that they should speak differently may not have the desired effect. In fact, it might serve to harden their stance. After all, how would you feel if someone, even if they were clearly well-intentioned, set out to tell you what you should and shouldn't say about yourself?

Denying a student's voice is not the best way to get them to change their language.

An alternative method, a subtle method, is reframing. It works as follows:

- Listen to what the student says.
- Consider how you could reframe these words back to them, so they take on a different meaning.
- Speak the words to the student.

- If appropriate, draw their attention to the difference between their initial words and your reframed version.

Here are three examples of the technique in practice:

**Student 1:** I'll never be able to do this, so why bother?

**Teacher 1:** Not being able to do something is how we all start out. If we work at it together you'll start to get the hang of it.

**Student 2:** I just can't do it.

**Teacher 2:** Lots of people can't do it the first time they try. That's normal. Let's break it down and focus our efforts on one part of it to begin with.

**Student 3:** People don't change. You've got what you've got and that's it.

**Teacher 3:** You've definitely got what you've got, but that's just your starting point. I've seen you change this year, especially when you've focussed your effort on achieving a goal.

Notice how, in each case, the teacher is careful not to deny the voice of the student. When they reframe they show the student a different way to think about the matter in hand. This directs them away from fixed mindset premises, encourages them to be open to the possibility of change, and gives a different set of words with which they can think and speak.

When used regularly, reframing becomes a powerful tool through which to change the language of your classroom. It does this without stopping students from speaking or making them feel as if their words are not valued.

Drawing attention to the process of reframing means giving students an insight into why you are doing what you are doing. Over time, you can teach them how to use the technique themselves. This means they can reframe their own language – whether verbalised or thought – away from a fixed mindset perspective.

A nice feature of this is that you are giving students a self-regulation tool they can take with them and use in all sorts of situations – on the sports pitch, at home, at their next school, at university and beyond.

**Yet...**

The most well-known reframing technique connected to growth mindsets is use of the word 'yet' to alter the meaning of student statements:

- 'I can't do it' **becomes** 'You can't do it yet'
- 'There's no way I'll be able to solve this' **becomes** 'You haven't been able to solve it yet'
- 'I'll never be a decent fielder' **becomes** 'You're not the fielder you want to be yet'

This is a great technique. Simple, effective, easy to use.

There are a couple of caveats, though.

First, overuse can dull its impact. If students hear you reframing their language in this way again and again and again, they may come to see it as meaningless – just another thing that Miss does. To avoid this, I would caution against using the technique without restraint. By all means use it, just try to ration that usage so students don't become inured to it.

Second, students may respond negatively to your reframed statements. For example, 'You can't do it yet' may be met with: 'Easy for you to say' or 'No, I just can't do it'. Responses like this shouldn't come as a surprise. Changing how students think about themselves and their learning is an ongoing process. Using 'yet' to reframe language is just one step among the many that you will take on your journey to effect change.

Bring prepared for these kind of responses means they don't take you by surprise. It also means you can work out how to counter them. Personally, I find one of the best approaches is to acknowledge what the student says and to then explain why you reframed their language in the way you did. This sees you giving the student a clear rationale for your actions – an explanation of the underlying principles in which you believe and which you would like them to take on board.

This is difficult to argue against. It also conveys a powerful message. Namely, that the things you do in the classroom are underpinned by a serious, considered purpose and that this is predicated on your understanding of what is in students' best interests.

As a final point, it is worth noting that students can also benefit from examples of where your divinations come to pass. Imagine a maths class. Students are studying trigonometry. A group of pupils say they can't do it and will never be able to do it. The teacher uses 'yet' to rephrase their language.

Some weeks later the whole class have got the hang of trigonometry. At this point, the teacher takes a few minutes out to remind the class of what was said. This isn't done in the manner of 'I told you so'. Rather, it is done in a way which emphasises the role effort, persistence and the use of feedback play in successful learning. The point, as far as the teacher is concerned, is to give their students evidence of how they have changed in the past few weeks, and to tie this change to how you think about yourself as a learner.

**Mental Contrasting**

Our penultimate technique involves teaching students a structure through which to think about the future. It works as follows:

- **If** I want to play the piano, **then** I must practice every night.
- **If** I want to run faster, **then** I must do two sprint training sessions a week.
- **If** I want to get full marks on my spelling test, **then** I must practice my spellings once in the morning and once in the evening.

If...then...

This is called mental contrasting. The contrast is drawn between what is desired and what needs to be done to make that desire a reality.

The technique helps students make the connection between what they want and what they need to do to get the thing in question. It ties achievement of desires to the targeting of effort in pursuit of those desires. It makes goals a function of the processes which come before them. It defines the aim and then sets out the path.

You can see how this promotes persistence and determination. How it reflects the central tenets of a growth mindset.

One of the greatest benefits of this technique is that it helps students to sketch a path between where they are now and where they want to be. This path is often difficult for them to see. Hence why cries of 'I can't do it' or 'I'll never be any good at this' frequently sound so plaintive – so definite in their confirmation of what cannot come to pass.

You can train students in how to use mental contrasting in a number of ways. Here are three examples:

- Make the technique a regular feature of your lesson starts. Use it to frame what students are going to do and then encourage them to make a note of this, discuss it or speak it aloud to you in a game of call and response. For example, you might start a lesson by introducing the topic and then saying: If we're going to challenge ourselves today, then we need to be ready to attempt every extension task we see.
- Show students how the technique works and then ask them to use it as the basis of target-setting or target implementation. In the first case, students set their own targets, based on a self-assessment and in the form of 'If...then...' In the second case, the teacher gives students targets and they then use the 'If...then...' structure to state how they are going to successfully implement these.
- During activities, circulate through the room. Identify any students who are stuck. Help these students by giving them feedback in the form of 'If...then...' For example: 'If you want to improve the story, then you might think about looking at your use of adjectives'. You might want to draw students' attention to the structure of your feedback as you give it. Or, you might want to make a point of this later on – after they have successfully implemented your advice.

## Metaphors and Similes

We conclude this chapter by turning to metaphor and simile. This does not end our engagement with language – that will run throughout the book. But it does signal the end of our exclusive focus on it.

How do you tell people about your internal world?

You cannot point to it. You cannot see it. Nor can anyone else. You can't jab your thumb in the direction of your feeling of happiness and say 'There it is, that's what I'm talking about'.

We can do this, of course, when discussing the external world in which we all live. 'Look at this beautiful poppy,' you say, and your friend looks at the poppy to which your finger is pointing. 'Smell this,' you tell your partner, and, dutifully, they take a whiff of the fresh mint you've bought.

But what do we do when the thing we're talking about cannot be seen?

One of the ways we overcome the problem is by using figurative language to communicate information about our internal states. This is not the only thing we do, but it is the one we will look at here.

'I've a raging headache.'

'You light me up.'

'I feel like a million dollars.'

Each example demonstrates how metaphor, symbol and simile act as a bridge. A way to convey information about what other people cannot see and cannot feel (I can feel pain, but I cannot feel your pain. I can empathise with your pain, but I cannot feel the pain that you possess).

This way of thinking plays a role in how we conceive of our subjective experience, including our minds and our sense of self. Nearly all of us use metaphor and simile to describe who we are, how we feel and what we think is possible. Maybe not all the time, but definitely some of the time. For example:

'My mind's starting to melt.'

'I'm like a robot when I'm in this place.'

'Me doing that would be like a duck trying to drive a tractor!'

You can use metaphors and similes to change how your students think about themselves as learners and what they perceive it is possible to achieve. You can give them a different language with which to speak.

Here are some growth mindset metaphors and similes to illustrate the point:

- Your brain is like a muscle – it gets stronger the more you use it.
- Feedback is your friend; it's there to help you.
- Effort is a vector – it needs direction as well as size.
- Challenges are brain food.
- Mistakes are the building blocks of understanding.

You can use these or come up with your own. Either way, you'll be presenting your students with a different way in which to think and talk, giving them growth mindset language they can return to again and again.

**Key Points to Take Away**

1) When looking to develop growth mindsets in the classroom, language is the place to start.

2) Give students growth mindset vocabulary with which to think and talk.

3) Use stories to convey growth mindset ideas.

4) Pay attention to the language students use – and to your own.

5) Model growth mindset language use, including techniques such as mental contrasting.

# Chapter Three – Changing How Students Perceive Mistakes

## Introduction

If a student believes intelligence, talent and ability are fixed, then it is more likely they will perceive mistakes and failure in a negative light. This, in turn, will make them less inclined to persist when things get challenging – because persisting involves making mistakes, failing and trying again in spite of this.

When promoting growth mindsets, we want to change how students perceive mistakes and failure. By doing this, we seek to alter the perceptions which underpin how they think about learning, and about themselves as learners.

Our ultimate aim is to help students see mistakes as a useful part of the learning process. This might result in them perceiving mistakes as a good thing (because of the information to which they give rise) or in a neutral light (as an inevitable part of all learning). But it will almost always lead us to dispel, or at least minimise, any negativity they might associate with mistake-making, as well as the costs they perceive as being attached to failure.

The rationale behind a positive view of mistakes is simple: When learning something new, it is to be expected that we will make mistakes. The mistakes we make give us access to information. We can use this information to change what we do and how we think. Or, to put it another way, to help us learn.

A child who goes through school without ever making a mistake will not have learned as much as they could have done. Nor will their thinking have been sufficiently challenged.

Failure sits alongside mistake-making. While there are subtle differences between the two, we can think of them as being largely similar for the purposes of this chapter. When students fail, they find themselves in a situation where they need to persist if they want to move forwards. Part of this persistence must involve putting the emotional experience of failure to one side and looking objectively at what has happened and why. They can then use this information to improve, helping them to succeed where once they had fallen down.

The principles are the same. Failure happens. It's an inevitable (natural) part of the learning process. It's no big deal. By looking at why we failed we gain information we can use when we try again. By trying again we get closer to being successful...and so on.

In the remainder of this chapter we will look at a range of different strategies, activities and techniques you can use to help change students' attitudes to mistakes and failure. I would suggest choosing one or two of the entries to try out and adapting them to suit your teaching style. You should then persist with them over a number of months. This approach will help you to establish new patterns of thought and action in your classroom, and reflects the fact that this takes a while, with change rarely happening overnight.

**Mistake Quotas**

Consider this set of instructions, which a teacher could display at the start of their lesson:

**'In this lesson I expect you to make a minimum of 3 mistakes. If you get half-way through and haven't made any mistakes, you need to ask me to make the work more challenging for you. At the end of the lesson we will spend five minutes reflecting on what we learned from our mistakes and deciding whether the lesson was sufficiently challenging.'**

This is a mistake quota. The teacher is giving students a license to make mistakes. Mistakes are being actively encouraged. The explicit message is that all students need to make mistakes during the lesson. The implicit message is that mistakes are a good thing – something the teacher wants to see.

Using this technique regularly means habituating students into a way of working in which mistakes are seen as desirable and useful. It also draws the link between making mistakes and having your thinking challenged. Students are expressly told that there is an important relationship between these two things. The message is very clear: mistakes are one of the indicators that the work set by the teacher is at the right level.

You can adapt the technique by focussing on individual activities instead of the lesson as a whole. For example:

**'While writing your essay I expect you to make at least three significant changes, based on what you feel you haven't got right first time round. When you've finished your essay, write me a note explaining where you made mistakes and how you improved on your first attempt.'**

Here we have a significant task (writing an essay) with a mistake quota appended. This influences how students approach the task, what they do during the task, and how they perceive mistake-making throughout.

One important point to note is that you may need to define what mistakes look like when using this technique. So, for example, in the essay writing just mentioned, we might tell our class to focus on major mistakes such as lack of clarity, incorrect use of key vocabulary and limited evaluation, rather than on minor issues such as spelling mistakes.

The point is to ensure students are attending to mistakes which matter more in the wider context of their learning – and which you want them to focus on. A brief explanation when introducing the quota, allied to some modelling, is nearly always sufficient to achieve this.

**Reframing Mistakes**

Reframing sees us taking something students say, something they think or something with which they are familiar and recasting it in a different light. It is usually a semantic exercise, in which we seek to change the meaning of something by altering how it is presented.

Reframing mistakes means re-presenting them to students in a positive light. This gives them a different way in which to think and talk about mistakes. In addition, we redefine the norms of our classroom, specifying, as we do, how we would like mistakes to be viewed and spoken about.

Here are some examples of how to reframe mistakes:

**Student A:** It's just wrong, isn't it, so why bother?

**Teacher:** I wouldn't expect you to be getting it right yet – we've only just started. Getting it wrong is the first step to getting it right, so let's see what we can learn from the mistakes.

**Student B:** It's no good, miss. Look at all the errors. I can't do it.

**Teacher:** Errors are a good thing, Sarah. They show us where we need to focus our efforts to improve. If you weren't making any errors, the work would be too easy. And I want my lessons to be challenging for you!

**Student C:** Why should I try again if all I'm doing is being wrong all the time?

**Teacher:** Well let's use being wrong as our starting point, Errol. If we know where we went wrong then we know what we need to think about to get better. We'll sit down together and discuss how to get it right next time.

In each example, the negative connotations students attach to mistake-making are not outright denied. Doing this could cause conflict and make the student feel their voice is being shut down. Instead, the teacher reframes the language in which mistake-making is couched.

This provides an alternative model through which the student can think. It also sees the teacher setting the agenda. How they reframe student language sets the scene for what comes next – persistence and trying again. Without reframing, it's more likely the students in question will give up. This reinforces the negative narrative in their minds, creating a self-fulfilling prophecy.

In summary, reframing sees the teacher giving students a different way to think about mistakes, without denying their voice or sense of agency. It signals a positive perspective on mistakes and, through doing so, offers a way forward which leads to growth, development and learning.

### Good Mistakes

A more general reframing technique involves redefining mistakes made in the classroom as 'good mistakes'. This can take one of two forms.

First, you can redefine all mistakes as 'good mistakes'. This results in a shift in the language of the classroom. The hope is that a concomitant shift will follow in the minds, thoughts and actions of your students. To achieve this, it is best to consistently explain to students *why* mistakes are good mistakes. Otherwise, they may see the linguistic change as purely superficial, as opposed to what it really is – a genuine attempt to redefine what mistakes are and what they give rise to.

Second, you can redefine a certain subset of mistakes as 'good mistakes'. This means choosing to rename only some mistakes. The most obvious example here is to refer to mistakes which have a significant impact on learning as 'good mistakes'. Commonly, this means misconceptions.

So, for example, we might find a maths teacher deciding to call any misconceptions students make 'good mistakes' before using these as teaching points. In addition, the teacher would be sure to explain to her students why she is calling these mistakes 'good mistakes', drawing their attention to the reasoning which underlies the change.

When using either of these approaches you should aim to be consistent over time. It may take some students a while to become accustomed to seeing and talking about mistakes in this ostensibly novel manner. In addition, it is helpful to refer to mistakes you make as 'good mistakes'. These can be accidental or deliberate. Either way, you are showing students that we all make mistakes and that we can all choose how we perceive them – as opportunities or threats.

A nice starter activity through which to reinforce the idea sees you collecting together a set of good mistakes, displaying these on the board and asking students to explain why they are good mistakes. Here, the emphasis is on getting students to articulate why the mistakes are mistakes. In so doing, they analyse the thinking which has given rise to them, before outlining what the correct approach ought to involve.

Thus our maths teacher might start a lesson by displaying the following on the board:

'Take a look at these good mistakes, then discuss with your partner why they are good and what we can learn from them'

**Good Mistakes:** $10 + 4 = 104$     $20 \times 2 = 22$        $300 - 1000 = 700$

In this example, each of the good mistakes illustrates a common error or misconception connected to the relevant type of calculation. The mistakes reveal information about the processes from which they arise. This is information we can learn from, teach from and use to avoid making such mistakes in the future. It is also information which helps us to better appreciate our own understanding of the processes in question.

**Trial and Improvement**

Promoting trial and error means promoting the idea that mistakes are OK. It also means diminishing the costs of failure. If students know we expect them to try things out, make mistakes and then try again, their perception of the costs of failure will likely change.

When introducing a greater degree of trial and error into your lessons, you might like to rename it 'trial and improvement'. The logic is clear; it echoes the points made in the previous section looking at good mistakes.

You can weave trial and improvement into your lessons in all sorts of ways. Here are seven examples:

- Include a trial and improvement success criterion when asking students to complete an activity or create a piece of work. For example: I want to see evidence that you have tried and improved at least two different layouts before settling on your final leaflet design.

- Mark the working out that students do. This approach is common in maths. You may remember being asked to 'show your working' when you were at school. It can be extended across the curriculum.

- Discuss students' work with them during the 'working out phase'. For example, a dance teacher might circulate through the room while students are preparing a new routine. As he does, he discusses ideas with students and encourages them to try things out and then improve them.

- Give students time in which to test ideas and problem-solving strategies. For example, a geography teacher might ask students to design a tourism map of the local town centre but first give them a testing period in which trial and improvement is the focus, rather than the creation of the map.

- Regularly include planning time in activities and teach students how to use this. For example, show them how to try ideas out and then improve them, explaining why this matters and how it leads to better end products.

- Encourage the use of supplemental thinking tools which give students space to try things out. The three simplest examples are mini-whiteboards, scrap paper and rough books. Each provides an additional space in which trial and improvement can happen, in advance of the main piece of work.

- Build verbal rehearsal into your activities. This sees students discussing and debating ideas prior to using them (either in writing or practically). Discussion provides a space in which students can edit, refine and clarify their thinking prior to using it – a clear example of trial and improvement.

**Mistake Logs**

Mistake logs allow teacher and student to keep track of mistakes over time. This also means the results of those mistakes can be tracked. Why is this a good idea? Three reasons. First, it helps students to see the connection between making mistakes and learning. Second, it lets students monitor how their mistakes have helped them to learn. Third, it means the teacher can see if students are making the same mistakes again and again, and therefore not learning from them.

To create a mistake log, open a new PowerPoint document, change the page layout to portrait and insert a table with four columns and ten rows. Label the columns as follows:

**Column 1** = Date

**Column 2** = What was the mistake?

**Column 3** = What caused you to make the mistake?

**Column 4** = What did you learn from the mistake?

Create copies of the document and hand these out to students. Now the whole class has a tool through which they can keep track of, reflect on and analyse the most important mistakes they make.

I say 'most important mistakes' because the log will lose some of its impact if it is used to record any and every mistake. Better instead to have students focus on those 'good mistakes' which reveal a lot of useful information. This way, the log develops a greater sense of meaning than if it gets filled up with simple, easy-to-rectify mistakes.

Of course, it would be wrong to assume that students will use their logs as you intend unless you give them guidance.

To this end, I would suggest introducing the logs to students, explaining why you want to use them, what the benefits will be, and how they can be best applied. In addition, it is worth planning reflective plenaries at particular points in the term during which students fill in their logs, discuss their entries with a partner, and share what they have observed with you and the rest of the class.

Creating an exemplar mistake log when first introducing the technique is also a good idea. This gives students a reference point for filling in their own logs. Something they can imitate and then internalise.

Finally, a different option involves creating a whole class mistake log. Here, the aim is to make the process of identifying and reflecting on mistakes a shared endeavour. One good way to do this is to create a wall display entitled: 'Our Best Mistakes'. You can then lead your class in adding to this through the course of the year. It will become a record of the good mistakes – and concomitant learning – to which your lessons give rise.

## Mistake Discussions

Discussing mistakes means giving them status. After all, we do not discuss things we deem unworthy of conversation. In the classroom, discussion occupies a different position compared to other areas of life. There is an underlying assumption that its role is always educational, at least to some extent.

Therefore, if we encourage the discussion of mistakes, if we plan to include mistake discussions in our lessons, we signal to students that mistakes are a good thing, that they are intimately connected to learning, and that we want them out in the open, rather than hidden away or avoided at all costs.

Here are five ways you can include mistake discussions in your lessons:

- Following on from the starter activity outlined in the 'good mistake' section above, plan to regularly begin your lessons with these tasks. Ensure a significant discussion element is included. For example, you might ask students to discuss why certain mistakes are good mistakes, to compare and contrast different mistakes, to discuss how mistakes can be fixed, or to discuss how they would teach other students to avoid certain mistakes.

- Present your class with a piece of exemplar work containing a number of key mistakes. Display this on the board and hand copies out so that students have one between two. Lead a discussion in which you and the class discuss the work, identifying and fixing the mistakes you find.

- Present students with an exemplar exam script containing a series of mistakes, along with a mark-scheme. Invite them to work through this in pairs, using the mark-scheme to identify and correct the mistakes. Conclude the activity by asking students to draw out what they and the class can learn from each of the mistakes identified. If you have time, you might like to develop this by asking students to make a guide to the exam paper called 'Good Mistakes and How to Avoid Them'.

- If you use show and tell with your students, why not turn one iteration of this into 'Mistake Show and Tell'? Doing so is easy. Simply tell students that you want to hear about the best mistake they ever made – and that this means the mistake that taught them the most, whether they made it in school or somewhere else, such as at karate club. Kick things off by modelling an example yourself.

- At the beginning of a topic, provide students with an overview of what they will be studying in the form of a handout. Invite them to look at this in pairs and to predict some of the mistakes they think they might make during the unit of work. Develop this into a whole-class discussion and capture student ideas by creating a 'mistake-predictions document' based on the five boldest or most common predictions put forward. Return to this through the course of the unit and use it as the basis of further mistake discussions.

**Eliciting and Teaching Away from Misconceptions**

One of the most important reasons for changing student attitudes to mistakes is that we need these mistakes out in the open if we are going to teach away from them. If the mistakes students make don't come out, it is likely they will continue making them in future. This may result in the impact of the mistakes being compounded.

As an example, imagine a student who is labouring under a misconception over what alliteration means. If the teacher can get this mistake into the open early on, then they can teach away from it. This helps the student to better understand alliteration and moves them away from their mistaken way of thinking.

However, let us imagine that the mistake does not get out into the open, meaning the teacher cannot teach away from it. Further down the line, the student makes use of the concept in an extended piece of writing. Perhaps in response to an exam question. Here, the impact of the misconception is compounded. Everything the student writes about alliteration rests on a faulty understanding of the term.

This vignette illustrates why eliciting mistakes is in the best interests of the teacher and the student, whereas keeping them locked away is, ultimately, to no one's benefit.

A few points follow:

First, when trying to change student perceptions of mistakes, talk them through this process, either individually or as a whole class. Explain why you want to know about their mistakes, why you want them out in the open and why this is a good thing for everybody. Use examples such as the one above to illustrate what this means in practice. You might also like to call on your prior experience in order to offer further exemplification of the point.

Second, when you are planning, teaching and assessing, you can do so with the aim of eliciting and teaching away from mistakes in mind. This might lead you to plan assessments, for example, which are more focussed on common misconceptions and recurring areas of uncertainty. Or, it might cause you to circulate more often during whole-class activities, and to do so with the sole aim of identifying mistakes from which you can teach away.

Third, increasing your use of diagnostic questioning creates more opportunities for mistakes to come out into the open. Diagnostic questions are those questions which aim to diagnose the current extent of student knowledge and understanding. For a selection of techniques through which you can elicit information from the whole class at the same time, see my Whole-Class Feedback Guide, available for free at www.mikegershon.com

**Hinge Questioning**

A specific example of diagnostic questioning is hinge questioning. This type of questioning focuses on the most important misconceptions and mistakes students might make in a given topic. Whereas diagnostic questioning is generally broad, requires little planning and can be applied in any situation, hinge questioning is specific, needs to be developed in advance and is usually only relevant to one situation. It works as follows:

The teacher identifies the key piece of information on which learning hinges. For example, in a lesson looking at photosynthesis, the key piece of information would be what photosynthesis is. If students have a sound understanding of this, they can move on securely. If they don't, they will move on working from a basis of uncertainty. This, therefore, is the key point on which learning hinges.

Having identified the hinge point, the teacher then constructs a question designed to test student understanding and to draw out common mistakes and misconceptions. Here is an example:

**Hinge Question:** What is photosynthesis?

**A)** The process by which plants convert sunlight into food.

**B)** The way in which plants get their food.

**C)** The process by which plants convert light energy into chemical energy.

**D)** The way plants turn carbon dioxide into food and oxygen.

The correct answer is **(C)**. However, the other answers may all seem plausible to students. Indeed, this is the point. Contained in the incorrect answers are common misconceptions and mistakes that we would expect some students to make. The point of the hinge question is to draw these out, so that we can teach away from them.

Compare the above example to some diagnostic questioning around photosynthesis:

- What can you tell me about photosynthesis?
- How would you define photosynthesis?
- What makes photosynthesis important?
- Is photosynthesis about making food? Why?

These are good questions, but they do not get to the heart of the matter as swiftly and precisely as the hinge question does. In addition, you can pose the hinge question to the class as a whole, making it easy to quickly identify those students who need further support and those who are ready to move on.

In summary, eliciting mistakes and teaching away from these is always a sound part of any teacher's practice. A combination of diagnostic and hinge questioning will help you to do this effectively. Making the elicitation of mistakes a central feature of your teaching helps normalise the idea of mistake-making in student minds, thus changing their attitude to mistakes and helping them to develop growth mindset habits.

**Mistake Rehearsal**

The great advantage of rehearsal is that when the time proper comes around you already know what you need to do. When it comes to making mistakes we can teach students how to respond by taking them through a process of rehearsal. This lets them reap the benefits of rehearsal in the context of mistake-making.

As teachers we are experienced in responding to mistakes – be that in relation to teaching or in relation to learning. Our students, however, are not yet so experienced. Mistake rehearsal is all about closing the gap. You can go about this in all manner of ways, including:

- Planning activities which are so challenging that all students will make mistakes, then leading students in an analysis of what happened, why it happened and the different responses it elicited throughout the class. You and your students can then rank the efficacy of these responses from best to worst, creating a toolkit of good responses which everybody can practice applying in the future.

- Modelling examples of how to respond positively to mistakes. For example, a PE teacher introducing students to long jump for the first time might begin by taking them through a series of common mistakes – running up too fast, overstepping the board, pulling out of the jump – and narrating the thought process they would go through, as an expert, in response to each of these mistakes.

- Modelling examples of general or subject-specific problem-solving strategies before giving students an opportunity to practice applying these. For example, an English teacher might model an approach to rewriting sentences which don't make sense. Students can then apply this technique whenever they make a similar mistake (though this may require some prompting from the teacher on the first few occasions).

- Setting students the task of creating a decision tree showing what they will do when faced with mistakes. For example, a history teacher might ask students to create decision trees showing how to respond to a series of specific mistakes – such as running out of time in an exam, overlooking a key point in an argument, or incorrectly analysing a source.

- Asking students to predict what mistakes they might make before suggesting how they could respond positively in each case. For example: by trying a different problem-solving strategy; by asking for help; or by looking back through their work to identify the cause of the mistake.

**Key Points to Take Away**

1) Mistakes and failure are an important part of learning.

2) Students who fear mistakes and failure, and do their best to avoid it, are less likely to persist in the face of challenges.

3) We can change how students perceive mistakes and failure.

4) Doing this takes time and requires persistent use of a few key techniques.

5) Lots of techniques are available, as seen above. You should choose the ones which work for you and stick with them.

# Chapter Four – Targeting Student Effort

## Introduction

Students operating under a growth mindset are more likely to see effort as a path to mastery. For them, there is a connection between effort and growth. This gives effort meaning. Meaning very often underpins motivation which, in turn, drives behaviour.

Consider, in contrast, a student who has a fixed perspective. For them, intelligence, talent and ability are definite and unchanging. This student is unlikely to see effort as a path to mastery. Mastery is instead something you either have or do not have. It cannot be gained, but simply is. Therefore, effort has less meaning, less purpose.

You will no doubt have encountered students who think in these different ways. On the one hand, some students persist in the face of difficulties, driven by an underlying belief that application of effort can lead to change and growth. On the other hand, some students quickly give up and, when questioned, fire off comments such as: 'What's the point, anyway?' 'I'll never be able to do it, so why bother?' and 'I'm no good at it so I don't see why I should have to try.'

Our aim – the aim of this book – is to find ways through which to cultivate a growth mindset perspective in all students. When it comes to effort this means we want all students to see effort as a path to mastery. From this we hope that certain behaviours will follow. Namely, persistence, increased focus and a belief that learning and development is possible for all, in any situation.

But this chapter is not just about effort. It is about targeted effort.

Why?

Because effort on its own is not enough. The statement 'effort is the path to mastery' rests on an unspoken assumption: that effort needs to be targeted, preferably with useful input from the teacher or through self-reflection and analysis.

Promoting growth mindsets is therefore not just about promoting the primacy of effort. It is about promoting the primacy of targeted effort. Effort that has a direction and a purpose. That is underpinned by supportive guidance or a clear rationale related to learning in general or the specific goal an individual student is seeking to achieve.

The practical strategies which follow all focus on this nuanced idea of effort.

Each gives you a way to help students target their efforts. In so doing, they will make better progress than would otherwise be the case. And they will get to see first-hand evidence of the efficacy of targeted effort, reinforcing the argument that a growth mindset perspective is a more accurate reflection of the reality of learning.

**Effort is a Vector**

One way to make the distinction between useful and useless effort is to compare a person running on the spot to a person running towards a finish line. They might both expend the same amount of energy, but the relative usefulness of this differs greatly. The person who runs on the spot engages in much exertion, only to find themselves exactly where they started. The person who runs towards the finish line uses the same amount of effort, and ends up having achieved a goal.

This metaphor is a helpful way to show students what targeted effort means and why it is important.

When it comes to the classroom, we can say that effort is a vector. By this we mean that it has size and direction. For the person who runs on the spot, their effort has size only. For the person who runs towards the finish line, their effort has size and direction. Another way to think about this is that their effort has size and purpose.

A few points follow.

First, it is important that effort has meaning in your classroom. If the term remains vague and ambiguous it is less likely students will target their efforts effectively. It will also be harder for them to understand what you mean by effort and how effort makes itself known in the learning process.

Second, a good way to help students understand what you mean by effort, and what targeted effort involves, is to use a metaphor such as the one above. Of course, other metaphors are available. But whichever metaphor you settle on be sure to use it consistently so that students gain the clearest understanding possible of what you are trying to convey.

Third, it is helpful to clarify for students what targeted effort may involve in specific terms. This sits in complement to the general description provided through your guiding metaphor. Here are some examples to get you started:

- Using different strategies to try to solve problems.

- Using trial and error as a way to deal with challenges.

- Using success criteria to direct what you do during an activity.

- Asking for feedback on how to improve and then applying this to your work.

- Focussing on the task in hand and reminding yourself to refocus if/when your mind starts to wander.

In each of these examples something is directing student attention. This is either the student themselves through recourse to self-regulation, or information provided by the teacher – such as the feedback and the success criteria.

Overall then, this first strategy is all about helping students to understand what targeted effort involves both in a general sense and in a specific sense. Armed with this information they will be better placed to successfully target their efforts and to see the positive results which follow.

**Defining and Modelling Effort**

The most effective use of the term 'effort' always comes when teacher and students have a shared understanding of what is being referred to. This follows on from our previous point. We can further clarify the meaning of effort in students' minds by defining and modelling it in the context of the classroom.

Here are four examples of how to do this. The first two concern defining effort, the second two focus on modelling it:

- Decide on a definition of effort which fits what you want students in your class to be doing. For example, my definition would be: Effort in our classroom means you are focussing your mind on the work we are doing. Then, develop this definition by coming up with specific examples for different situations.

For example: Effort in our classroom means paying attention to whoever is speaking. Effort in our classroom means trying different strategies when you get stuck, then asking for help if you still can't do it. Effort in our classroom means using feedback to change what you do and why you do it.

Finally, share this with your students. You can use the definition repeatedly through the year, returning to it, and using the specific examples, as and when appropriate.

- Set up a discussion activity near the beginning of the year during which you come up with a definition of effort as a whole class. If you choose to use this technique, be sure to guide the class in their thinking so as to avoid the pitfalls of defining effort too broadly, of failing to consider the importance of targeted effort, and of not giving clear examples of what effort looks like when translated into specific situations.

- One of the best ways to model effort is to show students what it looks like in individual activities. For example, imagine a Design and Technology teacher has set their students the task of designing a Christmas gift which they will later make and try to sell at the school fair. The teacher models what effort will look like in the design process before giving students the signal to start. They do this by showing how they would go about the task, narrating their thinking and indicating where and how they would focus their energies.

- Another effective modelling technique is to show students a piece of exemplar work and to draw out from this a series of salient points concerning targeted effort. For example, a Year 6 teacher might show their students an exemplar story, before indicating how the author has rewritten two sections, has focussed on including a high level of description, and has also changed the ending after deciding it wasn't sufficiently gripping. These three points then become highly specific models students can imitate or adapt to ensure they effectively target their own efforts.

**Paying Attention to Working Memory**

Working memory is limited. There is a general consensus among psychologists that it is limited to 7 pieces of information, plus or minus two. Working memory is what we use to process information in the moment. In any lesson we are asking students to constantly use their working memory to learn, think, and complete tasks.

If a student's working memory becomes overloaded they will likely run into difficulties. In this situation, effectively targeting effort becomes very difficult. Some students will have learned strategies through which to overcome this. For example, they may store some information on scrap paper, freeing up space with which to think.

For those students who haven't developed such strategies, however, an overloaded working memory may lead them to withdraw from the learning. This reaction is understandable. It can also reinforce any perceptions that effort is not a route to mastery and therefore serves no purpose.

As teachers, it is important we are alive to working memory. Paying attention to it means thinking about when our students might find themselves overloaded. It also means being aware that a student who looks as if they are withdrawing from the learning may be doing so because they have unknowingly reached the limit of their capacities at that point in time.

We can help students who find themselves in this situation in a number of ways, all of which make it easier for them to target their efforts:

1. Teach students strategies for freeing up space in their working memories. For example, writing things down on scrap paper, verbalising thoughts and chunking items together.

2. Scaffold the work. For example, by breaking a task down into a series of subtasks, by providing students with support in the form of a writing frame or by suggesting what students might do next.

3. Use questions to direct student thinking, taking them through a series of things one at a time. For example, you might first ask them what they were thinking about, then why they thought that, then why they became stuck, then what they need to know to move on and so forth.

4. Make students aware of what working memory is, how it works, what its limitations are and how to make best use of it. You can do this with the whole class or with individual students.

5. Further your own understanding of working memory by visiting the website of The Centre for Working Memory and Learning at the University of York: www.york.ac.uk/res/wml/

**Success Criteria**

Success criteria help students to target their efforts by giving them a clear understanding of what they need to do to be successful. Without success criteria, they may spend more time trying to work out what they should be doing than getting on with the task you have set.

An added advantage is that you can use success criteria to redirect student effort, should this wilt during the course of the lesson. Students can also use the criteria to check their own work – perfect if you build redrafting/improvement time into your activities – and as a basis for peer-assessment.

Here are five examples of how you can use success criteria to help students target their efforts:

- Supplement the tasks you set with three success criteria which students need to meet to be successful. Develop the idea by including two additional success criteria as challenges. These then act as an extension, pushing the thinking, and therefore the effort, of any student who gets onto them.

- Show students a piece of exemplar work and highlight the sections which connect to the success criteria you are asking them to meet. Extend the activity by handing out copies of the exemplar work and asking students to assess how effectively this meets the various criteria. Then, challenge them to surpass this in their own work.

- Encourage students to use the success criteria you provide as guides when they are planning and executing their own work. For example, a Food Technology teacher might set three success criteria – one based on preparation, one based on creation and one based on attention to detail. He could then encourage his students to focus on each of these in turn as they move through a cooking activity.

- Set students an activity and explain that there are four success criteria you want them to meet. Reveal the first two and then indicate that you will reveal the others during the course of the activity. Do this at the times you feel are most appropriate – and watch as students have to reassess how they are targeting their efforts, and make changes in response to the new information you've shared.

- Train students to self-assess their work at specific points using the success criteria you provide. For example, half-way through an activity, just before the end and after they have finished. Highlight the relevance of each self-assessment. For example, half-way through means ensuring you are on track, just before the end means you can make any alterations before you finish and after you have finished means you can reflect on what went well and what you might need to improve next time.

**Instant Feedback**

Feedback of any kind gives students information they can use to change, alter and adapt what they do. Instant feedback means students can do this in the moment – hence why it can be a particularly good way through which to target student efforts. To illustrate, consider this example:

In a gymnastics lesson, the teacher has asked students to create a routine involving a series of different elements – rolls, stretches and jumps. Students are working in groups of three. They come up with their routines together, then perform them individually and give each other feedback. The activity lasts for around fifteen minutes and the teacher has made clear that students need to perform and improve their routines at least three times. There is also an extension activity lined up for anybody who feels they have perfected their routine within the time limit.

As the activity takes place, the teacher walks through the sports hall, moving from group to group. They observe what is happening, then provide instant feedback. For example:

**Teacher:** Jack, that's a nice transition from the floor but I think you've made it too easy for yourself. When I come back I want to see a higher level of difficulty, OK?

**Teacher:** Terence, give Marcus some support while he's trying to hold his legs up. That's it. Keep doing that during his repeat performances.

**Teacher:** Danny, I didn't see a jump in that routine. Remember what I said at the start of the activity? Tim, Saleem – you guys suggest a jump he can include then give him some feedback after he's worked it into the routine.

Imagine if the teacher continued to do this through the course of the fifteen minutes, ensuring they visited each group at least once. Now compare that situation to the same task, but with the teacher stood at the front of the room, observing but not intervening.

The former method, as illustrated, involves the teacher exerting a greater degree of control over how students are directing their efforts. The feedback he provides is instantaneous – and students are in a position to implement it without hesitation. They will also quickly see the results of their efforts – and be able to draw a connection between targeted effort and improved performance.

The principle can be applied across the curriculum. Pared down, it entails the teacher circulating during activities, providing instant feedback on what students have done, and then giving time for students to implement that feedback.

**Keyword Quota**

Here is a specific activity structure put together with the express intention of targeting student effort:

**Keywords:** Clutch; Gears; Steering Wheel; Acceleration; Brake; Indicators; Changing Lane; Mirror; Manoeuvre; Engine; Tyres; MOT; Tread; Exhaust; Motorway; Traffic Lights.

**Task:**

- You have three minutes to write a piece on the topic of 'Driving.'
- Your minimum keyword quota is six.
- No lists or bullet points are allowed.

As you will note, the activity has been designed in such a way that student attention is heavily directed, causing pupils to attend closely to the specified topic, and to do so in a way which is highly circumscribed.

The example is generic. We could replace the topic of driving with anything – trees, nuclear fission, the politics of Bismarck – and we could alter the caveats in various ways – extend the time limit, change the keyword quota, add in additional restrictions on top of no lists and no bullet points. This gives the activity a great deal of scope and demonstrates why it is essentially a vessel into which different content can be poured.

We can take a few things away from this.

First, the activity is a great one to have as part of your repertoire. It gives you a flexible way through which to target student effort (and it can be applied in non-logico-linguistic subjects as well, with a bit of tweaking).

Second, it demonstrates what can be achieved when we set out to plan an activity with the targeting of student effort at the forefront of our minds. Making this our central aim means we think slightly differently about how we might structure an activity and what consequences this might have for student thinking.

Third, and finally, it illustrates the general benefit of caveats as a tool through which to target student effort. Caveats are those riders we place onto a task, circumscribing the scope of what students are expected to do. In this case, the caveats are an essential part of the activity (a keyword quota of six; no lists or bullet points allowed). However, it is perfectly possible to append caveats to almost any activity. They then act as a supplement – and work in a way not dissimilar to success criteria – shaping how students approach and think about a task.

## Categories of Assessment

When a teacher looks at a piece of student work, they do so through learned eyes. It is as if they are wearing a pair of thought spectacles, crafted from their experience of teaching. They do not need to do the hard work of thinking through what constitutes success, failure, lack of effort, effective effort and all the rest of it. They know this. It is committed to long-term memory.

For these reasons, most teachers can pick up a piece of work and make a quick and highly accurate broad brush assessment of its quality.

If we ask students to assess their own work, or the work of a peer, we are asking them to do something which does not come as easily. The reason is simple. They do not have the same level of experience as we do. Nor do they have the same knowledge or understanding.

This is also why peer- and self-assessment are so useful. They help students to better understand what we take for granted – the criteria of assessment, the hallmarks of good work, and the separate elements which constitute success.

One of the main ways in which peer- and self-assessment fall down is lack of scaffolding. Students do not have the tools they need to make effective judgements. This, in turn, leads to ineffective application of effort. In some cases, it results in students making irrelevant or unhelpful judgements: 'I like the way you've coloured in the title'. In other cases, it causes students to withdraw or give up: 'I don't see why we need to do this, anyway. What's the point? Why don't you just mark our work?'

This can be avoided, and effort successfully targeted, by providing a set of categories students can use as the basis of their assessments. Here is an example:

## Task:

A picture of a butterfly is displayed on the board. Students are given ten minutes to copy the image as best they can.

64

**Peer-Assessment:**

The following categories are displayed:

Outline; Colour; Pattern; Shape; Line; Symmetry; Wings; Antennae; Body; Scale.

Along with the following instructions:

Swap your work with a partner. Look at their drawing and select one or two of the categories. Use these as the basis of your feedback. Tell your partner where they have succeeded and give them one thing they could do to improve. Remember to keep your feedback focussed on the category or categories you select.

The technique turns peer- or self-assessment from a potentially vague or ambiguous exercise into a highly-specific one. The categories give students access to your expertise and make it easier for them to give meaningful feedback. Everybody's effort is targeted as a result.

**Modelling, Prompting and Clueing**

If a student becomes stuck, we don't necessarily want to give them the answer. This undermines the beliefs we are trying to promote – that effort is a path to mastery and that persistence in the face of challenges is a good thing. At the same time, though, we know that there are many situations where, if we do nothing, the student in question may give up, withdraw or decide that there is no point continuing to try.

In these situations we can call on modelling, prompting and clueing. Each strategy presents a subtly different way through which to help students, without doing too much of the work for them. The help we provide gives them what they need to refocus their attention and to apply their effort in the direction of learning. Let's look at each in turn.

**Modelling.** This sees us giving students a model of how to do something, allowing them to copy, imitate or adapt what we present. For example, we might model how to complete a task, how to search for the answer to a question, or how to use trial and improvement to develop the quality of your work.

**Prompting.** This is less interventionist than modelling. It involves using prompts to spark student thinking. Here are some examples to illustrate the idea:

- What was that word we used earlier...?

- Is this a good time to return to the checklist?

- Can you remember what you told me last time you hit a problem like this?

In each of these examples we are not going so far as to provide students with a full-blown model of what to do. Instead, we are prompting them to think in a certain way or to go back a certain thing with which they are already familiar.

**Clueing.** This is the least interventionist of the three techniques. Clueing sees us giving students clues about what to do next or how to think. It is then up to the student to interpret the clues. Here are some examples:

- Try having a look at Page 16...see what you can find there.

- It could have something to do with refrigeration. I'm not saying for definite...but it might be worth thinking about.

- Well I think Bohr's work offers an interesting perspective. I'll leave the rest up to you.

Being aware of the differences between modelling, prompting and clueing ensures you are well placed to use the most appropriate technique for the student in front of you. This makes your interventions more effective, and lets you target student effort with a greater degree of skill.

### Strategy Sharing and Strategy Reflection

Right at the beginning of the chapter we spent some time thinking about the difference between running on the spot and running towards a finish line. This metaphor, we said, is a neat way of expressing the differences between effort which isn't targeted and effort which is.

One of the characteristics of many students operating under a growth mindset is that they persist in the face of challenges. But what form does this persistence take? What does it look like in terms of effort?

Well, one of the key things we tend to see – and you will undoubtedly be able to relate this to students you have taught – is students attempting a series of different strategies in an effort to reach their goal.

For example, a PE student might be trying to bend a free kick around a wall. They try this ten times, failing on each occasion. So what do they do? They start thinking about how they are approaching the ball, the part of the foot they are using to strike it, the point at which they make contact, the position of their standing leg.

Over the next fifty or sixty attempts they vary each of these factors, observing the results. Essentially, they are engaged in a process of trial and error in which they employ a variety of strategies, and make a variety of tweaks to what they are doing, in an effort to find a solution to the problem of bending the ball around the wall.

This is targeted effort. And we can take away two things to use in any lesson we teach.

First, strategy sharing is always welcome. It could be that you share strategies with your students, giving them different techniques to try. Or, it could be that you encourage students to share strategies with one another. Either way, the aim is to ensure that everybody in the class has options open to them when they hit a problem – and knows how to take advantage of these.

Second, strategy reflection is a useful way to get students thinking critically about the techniques they used when faced with a problem, and the results which sprung from this. You can make strategy reflection the focus of a plenary, or you can use it as a mid-lesson review, inserting it directly after an activity in which students have had to struggle in order to be successful.

Both of these techniques encourage students to think about the strategies they are using, the results to which these give rise and how they might alter their actions to better target their efforts in the future.

**Key Points to Take Away**

1) Not all effort is equal. Targeted effort is what we want to see in the classroom.

2) Promoting targeted effort means promoting the belief that effort is a path to mastery.

3) Defining and modelling effort minimises ambiguity, helping you and your and students.

4) Making students aware of the limitations of working memory, and the various things they can do to overcome this, gives them greater control over their own learning.

5) Developing a repertoire of scaffolding techniques, including those outlined above, gives you plenty of scope for effectively targeting student effort during any lesson.

# Chapter Five – Giving Great Feedback

## Introduction

Students operating under a growth mindset are more likely to see feedback as useful. This is because their thinking is animated by the central premise that intelligence, ability and talent are open to change. Therefore, feedback is seen as a route through which change can be effected. Feedback provides information the student believes they can use to alter their existing knowledge, understanding or skills for the better.

On the other hand, if a student is operating from the standpoint of a fixed mindset, then feedback may be perceived as a threat – something to be avoided or dismissed. The logic is simple. If you begin with the premise that intelligence, ability and talent are fixed, it follows that you do not believe you are in a position to change what you currently possess. Therefore, any feedback provided by an external source, such as the teacher, is asking you to do something you do not believe is possible.

But why is it that some students in this position see feedback as a threat? Why do some students shut down, or even physically recoil, when the teacher tries to give them feedback about their work?

One explanation is that the student perceives the feedback as a statement being made concerning what they lack, cannot do and do not have. The student, believing that talent, ability and intelligence are fixed, sees the feedback as something it is impossible to make use of. Therefore, the feedback is merely highlighting what they can't do – identifying a deficit – and this is then interpreted as an attack on the student's sense of self.

The point here is not what feedback is in objective terms – information the student can use – but how it is perceived, subjectively, by the student who is operating under a fixed mindset.

It is important to note that the efficacy of feedback will be severely eroded in such situations. If a student is not receptive to the information provided by the teacher – either verbally or in writing – then the influence of that information will be significantly diminished. In some cases, it will have no impact at all.

When seeking to develop growth mindsets in the classroom, one of the things we are trying to do is change how some students perceive feedback. We want them to see it in a positive, rather than a negative, light. Our aim is to shift the underlying principle on which their thinking rests, so that they feel comfortable receiving and using the feedback we provide.

The practical strategies which follow help you to achieve this goal. They focus on the twin aims of providing effective feedback and using feedback in such a way that it promotes the central premise of a growth mindset: that intelligence, talent and ability are open to change, and that the individual is always the prime mover in making that change happen.

**Understanding the Difference Between Trait-Based Praise and Feedback-Led Praise**

Here are some examples of trait-based praise:

- Great work from you – just as I would expect!

- You're amazing!

- You're so clever.

- I knew a clever girl like you would get it right.

- Great answer, genius.

In each case, the praise has been delivered with the best of intentions. The teacher's aim is to reinforce positive behaviour and to convey approbation to the student. However, praise of this type can have quite different effects from those intended. And, for this reason, it is better avoided. The best way to do this is to reframe such praise, so that it is feedback-led and not trait-focussed. Let us explore what this means.

In each of the examples above, there is a suggestion that the child possesses innate qualities or traits which cause them to be successful. Such suggestions imply that intelligence, talent and ability are fixed. That they are definite quantities contained within us.

This obscures the fact that every individual is in a position to learn. To alter their current intelligence, ability and talent through the application of effort and hard work. As noted in the chapter on targeted effort, energy directed in pursuit of a goal is most effective at achieving change. And what better way to direct student effort than by providing them with appropriate feedback?

Our primary aim thus becomes to avoid trait-based praise of the sort illustrated above. This is because we want to reinforce the tenets of a growth mindset in our classroom, rather than those of a fixed mindset.

This does not mean we shouldn't give praise, however. Far from it. Instead, we should be careful to ensure the praise we do give fits with the growth mindset perspective. In so doing, we will often find our praise taking on a more feedback-based form. Here are some examples:

1) Great work from you – just as I would expect!

**Becomes: Great work today – I saw how you kept going even when I increased the level of challenge.**

2) You're amazing!

**Becomes: You've done really well today, I liked the fact that you were prepared to try a different strategy when you hit an obstacle. Keep it up.**

3) You're so clever.

**Becomes: You're keeping your effort levels high every lesson. That's helping you to produce work of a really high standard.**

4) I knew a clever girl like you would get it right.

**Becomes: That's right – can you talk me through your answer? I'd love to hear how you worked it out.**

5) Great answer, genius.

**Becomes: That's a fascinating answer. Tell me more. What else do you think about the question?**

In each case, reframing changes the underlying message of the praise. The student hears a different perspective as a result. Different behaviour and different thinking is reinforced. Instead of the student believing that something inherent to them is the ultimate cause of their success, they come to understand that the things they do, the choices they make, and the effort they target is the driving force behind whether or not they are successful.

**Reframing Away From Trait-Based Praise**

There are other ways you can reframe away from trait-based praise. These include:

- Turning praise into questions.

- Identifying a set of growth mindset categories to use as a reference point.

- Using 'because'.

We'll have a look at each in turn.

Reframing praise into questions means changing the focus of the conversation. Instead of intimating that something has happened and this has garnered praise, we intimate that something has happened and wouldn't it be interesting to talk about it? The conversation is opened up, rather than closed down. Focus shifts to how the thing in question came about, or what it is, rather than its relative quality.

Here are the examples from above, reframed into questions:

1) Great work from you – just as I would expect!

**Becomes: What do you think about your work today? What made it good?**

2) You're amazing!

**Becomes: How did you get to that answer? Can you explain what you did?**

3) You're so clever.

**Becomes: This work shows a really high level of accomplishment. What do I need to do to make things more challenging for you?**

4) I knew a clever girl like you would get it right.

**Becomes: Can you tell me whether the answer's right or not? How would you try to prove that it is?**

5) Great answer, genius.

**Becomes: What makes that a good answer? And what would someone else have to do to reach the same answer?**

These are indicative – you could reframe each piece of trait-based praise in numerous ways. They all illustrate the same point, though. Turning praise into questions means turning the focus of the conversation onto thinking, learning and the processes which give rise to both.

Another technique to have in your locker is a set of growth mindset categories you can use to focus and direct the praise or feedback you give. For example:

- Targeted Effort

- Level of Challenge

- Persistence

- Metacognition

- Use of Feedback

- Response to Difficulties

- Use of Trial and Error

Storing these categories in your mind – or having them displayed on your wall for easy reference – means you are always in a position to reframe your praise so it accords with growth mindset principles. The categories provide a reference point, meaning you don't need to start from scratch on every occasion. You can also think of them as a set of growth mindset filters through which you can pass your praise, reframing it in the process so that it accords with your wider intentions.

For example, we might be tempted to say 'You're so clever' to a child in our class. However, we stop ourselves from doing this, pass the praise through the filter of targeted effort and say instead: 'I love how you've been focussing your mind on the task in hand throughout the lesson. It's really helped you to create some great work.' We're still giving praise but, crucially, we're reinforcing the behaviour which is constitutive of a growth mindset – persistent targeting of effort. Filtering our language through the pre-identified categories means we can do this at a moment's notice.

The final technique to mention here is using the word 'because' as a pivot point whenever you give praise. So, for example:

'That's great'; 'Super work'; and 'That's want I want to see' become:

1) That's great, **because** mistakes are a good starting point for learning.

2) Super work, **because** you kept going even though it didn't come straight away.

3) That's what I want to see, **because** trying out different strategies helps you to improve.

Obvious, I know. But easily overlooked, especially if you're in a hurry. Rest assured, though, slipping 'because' onto the end of any piece of praise will ensure you continue speaking and provide the student in question with a reason explaining why the praise has been given. And it is this reason that promotes the growth mindset tenets we are seeking to cultivate.

**Focussing on Processes**

Processes are inherent to students; the products they produce are external to them. Focussing on processes means giving students feedback about how they think and the things they do when creating work. This means sending a clear message that the things which comprise the student's mind are open to change.

In contrast, if we only refer to the products students create, then we may find ourselves inadvertently focussing their attention on things which are final, fixed and no longer a part of them. To illustrate this point, consider the differences between these two pieces of feedback:

(1) This is a great essay, Mark. My attention was held throughout. By the time I reached the conclusion I felt that I had a much better

understanding of the issues – even though I didn't necessarily agree with the perspective on which you settled. Well done.

(2) This is a great essay, Mark. I can see that you **spent time thinking about how to sequence** your argument. That helped to maintain the reader's interest – it certainly kept my attention throughout. In addition, the clarity of your writing suggests you **spent a reasonable amount of time analysing** the ideas before beginning to write. This makes life easier for the reader and conveys a sense of authority. Finally, there is your conclusion. I wonder, what made you settle on this interpretation? Let's discuss it next lesson – **I'm interested to hear your reasoning**.

Piece One looks like good formative feedback at first glance. And, in general terms, it is. But note how the second piece contains a number of references to the processes which underpinned Mark's creation of the essay (highlighted). In the first two cases, the feedback draws Mark's attention to the choices he has made and the effort he has targeted, praising this by linking it to successful outcomes.

In the third case, the process is again made central. Only, this time, some ambiguity is introduced. The teacher wants to know more – they want to think in greater detail with Mark about why he settled on his interpretation. This has the effect of making Mark appreciate that, while the essay is good, it could still be improved. There is still room to develop, to change and to try again.

Ultimately, this is what a focus on process takes us and our students towards. A realisation that continued improvement is possible, and, often, desirable. It doesn't mean we eschew final acknowledgement of merit – Piece Two above begins by praising what Mark has produced. But it does mean that we contextualise praise of products by referring to the processes which gave rise to them.

Used regularly, feedback of this type helps students to appreciate their own agency and the central role they can play in changing what they are capable of – whether in terms of knowledge, understanding, skills or a combination.

There is more to say on the topic of processes, and we will return to it at length in Chapter Eight.

## Feedback on Trial and Error

Trial and error is something we want to promote in our classrooms. It is an important way in which we learn. It is also a strategy with wide application. We can call on it in almost any circumstance as a way to overcome obstacles. Every trial in which we engage elicits information. We use this information in subsequent trials to alter what we do. Eventually, in most cases, we reach a satisfactory conclusion. Very often, this is a result of cumulative gains achieved over a series of trials.

As we know, students operating under a growth mindset are more likely to see trial and error in a positive light. This is because they do not fear mistakes, instead acknowledging the role they play in the learning process. The logic is simple. If you believe intelligence, talent and ability are open to change, then it makes sense to see trial and error as a tool through which to make change happen.

On the other hand, students operating under a fixed mindset may well seek to avoid trial and error. For them, it represents a threat. That threat is formed from the belief that getting something wrong is a mark of a deficit concerning the individual who has erred. This flows from the underlying belief that talent, ability and intelligence are fixed. If you get something wrong, it shows you up. Therefore you avoid situations (like using trial and error) where there is a risk of being wrong.

One of the ways we can promote the growth mindset perspective on trial and error is by giving feedback on the process. This serves three ends.

First, it draws students' attention to it. In so doing, it highlights that trial and error is something in which we, the teacher, have an interest. This reinforces the idea that we want to see trial and error being used in the classroom, at the same time as it denies the idea that we will be disappointed should students make errors as they attempt to complete their work.

Second, it signifies the importance of trial and error. After all, if trial and error wasn't important, why would we bother giving students feedback about it?

Third, it gives us an opportunity to help students think about and improve the quality of their trial and error. The feedback we provide directs student attention, at the same time as it gives them information they can use to make changes in the future. This raises the profile of trial and error in the student's mind. It also helps them to refine their use of it.

Here are five examples of where and when you might give this type of feedback:

- By marking and commenting on students' working as well as their end product.

- By giving verbal feedback during activities while students are trying things out.

- By praising students' use of scrap paper, rough books and mini-whiteboards to test ideas before putting them into practice.

- By drawing out distinctions between students' first and second attempts (or second and third attempts).

- By making it clear that you want to see mistakes, crossing outs and errors because these are part of students' thinking – and that is what you want to give feedback on.

**Feedback on Mistakes**

As with trial and error, so too mistakes.

Giving students feedback on mistakes means you raise the status of these at the same time as you diminish the costs students might perceive as being attached to them. Imagine two classrooms. In the first, the teacher ignores mistakes or, worse still, gives a negative response when students make them. In the second classroom, the teacher pays attention to mistakes, shows interest in them, uses them as teaching points and gives feedback on them.

The second classroom is to be preferred. It is the one in which learning takes centre stage.

With this in mind, here are five ways you can give feedback on mistakes:

- When marking student work, highlight one or two important mistakes or misconceptions. Give feedback on these, drawing students' attention to why they made these, what information they give rise to and how to avoid repeating the mistakes in future.

- If a student makes a mistake or airs a misconception during an activity, use this as a chance to open up a new discussion. As you do, highlight why making mistakes is often a good thing and thank the student for presenting you with a teaching opportunity.

- Share common mistakes or misconceptions with the class as a whole. For each one, explain the kind of feedback you would give to help a student change their thinking. As you do this, walk students through the process of analysing and learning from mistakes. Remember, the process of giving feedback on mistakes is as much about diminishing student fear of making them as it is about giving students access to useful information.

- Develop the previous point by asking students to examine common mistakes or misconceptions and to discuss what feedback they would give to a student who made them. For example, at the end of a topic you might collect together the most important mistakes and misconceptions made during the course of the unit, display these on the board and then invite students to work in pairs to produce exemplar feedback that could be given in response to each one.

- Turn the whole process on its head by deliberately making mistakes yourself and inviting students to correct you. Stress the fact that we all make mistakes and that this is a part of learning at any age. You might also like to ask students questions which help them to think about how they analysed the mistakes you made. This metacognitive questioning helps them attend to the general processes of analysing and learning from mistakes.

**Target Implementation Strategies**

So far we have thought about the provision of feedback. Now we must consider its implementation.

If students don't have time in which to implement the feedback you provide then that feedback is wasted.

Feedback only has an impact if it is used – not if it is dismissed, forgotten or overtaken by events.

If we want students to view feedback positively – as a useful tool in the pursuit of mastery and development – then we need to ensure they have ample experience of what feedback can give rise to when it is successfully implemented. For this reason, it is important that you make use of target implementation strategies in your lessons.

These are any and all strategies in which the primary focus is on students implementing the targets you have given them. A specific and well-regarded strategy you might have come across is D.I.R.T. We look at this in more detail below.

First, we can consider a range of other strategies you can use to ensure students are implementing the targets they receive:

- **Target Tracker Sheets.** This is a sheet stuck into the front of student books on which all major targets are recorded. Teacher and student can then refer to the sheet at the beginning of lessons and activities, helping to keep the most recent targets fresh in the mind.

- **Write/Do/Reflect.** Students write their target at the top of the page. They then do the activity the teacher has set, trying to implement the target as they go. Finally, they reflect on how successful they were – either in discussion with a partner or by writing a short paragraph at the end of their work.

- **Plan/Do/Reflect.** As above but with practical activities. Here the student reminds themselves of their target and plans how to implement it. They then attempt to execute their plan before reflecting on what happened and the extent to which they were successful. You can develop this into a virtuous circle whereby students try again after their reflection.

- **Feedback – Activity – Feedback – Activity.** The teacher plans a lesson following this structure. For example, the lesson begins with the whole class receiving feedback. The teacher then introduces an activity in which students can try to use the feedback. Once this is done the teacher provides additional feedback, giving students suggestions for how they might further improve their work. A second activity is introduced and students attempt to put the new feedback into action.

- **Mid-Lesson Target Review.** The teacher plans a mid-lesson review in which the focus is on reviewing targets and assessing how successful students have been in meeting these. This is a good way to remind students of their targets and to keep them in view as the lesson progresses.

## D.I.R.T.

D.I.R.T. – which stands for Directed Improvement and Reflection Time – is a target implementation technique which has become popular in recent years, with good reason. The premise is simple: set aside a specific period of the lesson in which everybody's focus is solely on the implementation of feedback, reflection on work previously completed, and improvement of that work where appropriate.

The idea gains its power from the fact that most teachers understand the utility of such a lesson segment, but also realise that without defining a period of time as being exclusively for this purpose then the demands of getting through the content are likely to take over.

To put it another way, planning D.I.R.T. into the lesson and putting a red box around it means we are much more likely to make sure it happens and that the time doesn't get eaten up by other, seemingly more pressing, demands.

Here are some examples of how you can include D.I.R.T. as part of your planning:

- **D.I.R.T. Starters.** Instead of introducing new content in your starter activities, plan to let students use this time to improve their work or to reflect on and discuss their most recent targets. This could be done at the start of every day in a primary school, or at the start of some lessons in a secondary school (bearing in mind that you might not want to do it at the start of every lesson).

- **D.I.R.T. Plenaries.** Plan extended plenaries in which students have to go back and improve their work. Supplement this with a list of different things they can focus on – or even a set of illustrative targets from which students can self-select.

**- Every nth lesson.** Plan D.I.R.T for every 3rd lesson or every 5th lesson, depending on how often you see students and the wider demands of the curriculum. For example, a Year 5 teacher might plan D.I.R.T. for every third Literacy lesson while a Year 11 geography teacher might plan it for every fourth lesson.

**- D.I.R.T. target lists.** Take in student books and mark these. Instead of writing individual targets, create a list of ten targets encompassing the various issues you identify in the class as a whole. Return the books at the start of the next lesson and display the list on the board. Invite students to select a target and give them time in which to implement it. Circulate as this happens, offering support and ensuring students choose suitably challenging targets.

**- D.I.R.T. before handing work in.** Set students a major piece of work to complete. Indicate that you will collect this in once it is complete. However, before you do this, announce that students will have time in which to improve their work. For example, this could be a twenty minute D.I.R.T. lesson segment with different areas highlighted on the board on which students could choose to focus their attention.

**Demonstrating the Impact of Feedback**

The strategies outlined in the previous two sections give a number of different ways through which to help students implement the feedback you provide. This makes it more likely they will see the impact of using your feedback.

And this is an important part of cultivating growth mindset traits across the board.

A student who believes that feedback is a threat will tend to avoid it. It is self-evident that this avoidance will include not trying to implement any feedback which is given. This creates a self-fulfilling prophecy.

Feedback is deemed as irrelevant, therefore it is ignored. Nothing changes and so the student's view that their talent, ability and intelligence are fixed is borne out by events. This confirms their original supposition that feedback is a waste of their time.

Demonstrating the impact of feedback means giving students strong evidence – often irrefutable – both of the greater accuracy of growth mindset thinking when it comes to reflecting reality and the general benefits which arise when we take account of feedback and use it to change our thinking.

You can demonstrate the impact of feedback by using the various strategies above and then drawing students' attention to what happens as a result. In each case, the aim is to make the connection in their minds between what they have done (used feedback provided to them, even if they didn't particularly want to) and what has come about because of this (a development in what they can do, what they know or what they understand).

Here are five further ways you can demonstrate the impact of feedback to your students:

- Through one-to-one discussions. This is particularly useful if you have specific students you want to target.

- By leading the whole class in a reflection looking at what you have studied in the year so far.

- By asking students to look back through their books and to identify where they have learned and developed as a result of the feedback they've received.

- By asking students to compare two pieces of work between which they have received feedback about how to improve.

- By asking students to highlight all the elements of a piece of work which have been influenced by the feedback they've received during the course of the year.

**Key Points to Take Away**

1) Feedback gives students access to information they can use to learn, grow and develop.

2) Students operating under a growth mindset are more likely to see feedback as helpful. Students operating under a fixed mindset may see feedback as a threat; they are also less likely to believe it can have an impact on their learning.

3) You can change the focus of your feedback so as to promote a growth mindset perspective.

4) You can do this by focussing on processes, trial and error and mistakes, as well as by avoiding trait-based praise and through reframing.

5) Feedback needs to be implemented. If not, it is unlikely to have much of an impact.

# Chapter Six – Thinking About Thinking

## Introduction

What are you thinking? How are you thinking about it? Are you in a position to observe the thinking that you do and to also analyse the efficacy of that thinking? To put it another way, do you find yourself in a position from which you can critique the processes which underpin your thinking, as well as the ideas, thoughts and behaviours to which they give rise?

Thinking about thinking, or metacognition, can take us to some conceptually tricky places. Particularly when we run out of usefully distinguishable words with which to specify the things to which we are referring. To illustrate the point, notice the potential for ambiguity in the title of this chapter. Does the repeated use of the word thinking mean we are signifying the same thing twice, or two different things, with their difference implied through the structure of the sentence, set alongside the context of this book?

While all of this is interesting stuff it may also seem a diversion. And it is, but only up to a point.

I draw some of the uncertainty and conceptual ambiguity to your attention to highlight that metacognition can be a difficult idea to convey to students. Therefore, it is worth deciding in advance how and to what extent you would like to use it in your classroom. This will save you time later on, as you will have already synthesised your understanding of the approach, making communicating with your students much easier.

The simplest definition is perhaps the most useful. When we say thinking about thinking, we mean that we want students to be critical of how they think, the strategies they use to try to solve problems, the decisions they make, and the ideas they seek to use as part of their learning.

But how does this connect to the development of growth mindsets? If we encourage our students to think about their own thinking, what benefits will this bring in terms of how they think more generally about intelligence, talent and ability?

There are a couple of answers.

First, if we encourage students to reflect on, critique and analyse their thinking then we are sending a clear message that this thinking is open to change. That it can get better. And that anyone can improve the quality of their thinking through the actions they take in relation to it. Encouraging metacognition means encouraging a belief in students of all ages that they have the power to influence how they learn, how they think and, as a result, the intelligence, talent and ability they possess at any point in time.

Second, getting students to think about their own thinking means getting them to verbalise, articulate and focus on the processes they make use of when they are learning. This helps them to realise that these processes are contingent and open to change – not fixed and eternal.

For example, a student who, through reflection, comes to understand that their approach to problem-solving in Design and Technology is far less refined than they thought, is also in a position to appreciate that how they think about problems is a part of themselves which is open to change, and that any changes made will impact on what they are able to do. This draws a powerful link in the student's mind between their own agency and the results which follow. Especially if highlighted by the teacher.

In summary, thinking about thinking helps all students to become more critical, reflective and analytical about their own learning. This, in turn, makes it easier for them to see their own abilities as being open to change, at the same time as it reinforces the link between individual agency and growth. With this in mind, let us look at some practical techniques you can use while teaching.

**Modelling Thinking**

In your classroom, you are the expert. This expertise extends beyond knowledge and understanding of the curriculum. It also includes knowledge and understanding of how to think – and how to learn.

Modelling thinking means giving students access to this expertise. This is to their benefit.

It provides them with a starting point for changing how they think. Initially, it is likely they will copy and imitate what you model. However, over time, they will come to internalise this before making it their own through modification and adaptation.

You can model thinking in many different ways. Undoubtedly you will already do it as part of your practice, although you might not necessarily conceive of what you are doing as the modelling of thinking (or, for that matter, the promotion of metacognition). Here are five examples to illustrate what it looks like:

- In a Year 3 class the teacher is working one-to-one with a student. They are looking at a maths problem. The teacher suggests one way the student might like to think about the problem. They model this, talking the student through what it would look like in practice. As they do, they also show the student by manipulating some plastic blocks, illustrating what this type of thinking can lead to.

- In a Year 6 class the teacher displays an exemplar piece of writing on the board. They wrote this in advance of the lesson. The teacher asks the class to discuss the merits of the piece. When they have finished, the teacher takes some thoughts from the group. Next, they start to talk the class through the thinking which underpins the piece of writing. The teacher explains the decisions they made, as well as the thought processes which led to the finished product.

- In a Key Stage 3 History lesson the teacher wants students to analyse a set of sources in a particular way. They model this method for the whole class, using a series of pre-prepared slides to show students the different steps they need to go through. The teacher then hands out a crib sheet detailing what the thinking looks like in practice, including a reiteration of the various steps.

- In a GCSE Maths lesson the teacher is introducing students to a new topic. This topic requires students to take a different perspective from what they are used to. As a result, the teacher begins by displaying a real-world problem and walking students through how a trained mathematician would go about trying to solve this. They then bring this modelling back to the classroom by contextualising it in light of the new topic.

- In an A Level PE lesson the teacher needs students to start thinking more strategically about their game management. To do this, they set up a game situation and ask students to play at half speed. The teacher then moves between them, narrating the kind of strategic thinking they want to see.

Notice how in each of these examples the same principle applies: the teacher is giving students access to their thinking. To their expertise. This gives them a model to imitate, modify and adapt. It also highlights the importance of thinking about thinking, and sends a clear message that all students' thinking is open to change.

**Reflective Questioning**

Reflective questioning causes students to look at what they have done during the course of a lesson, activity or sequence of lessons. The aim is simple. To help students assess and critique their own thinking, so they might better understand what they have learned and might also improve how they think in the future.

Reflection is the process by which we stop and consider that which we have done. We use the present to look critically at the past and, in so doing, to both reinterpret and reassess what we think we know.

This is reflection in its ideal form. It does not – and will not – always reach this level of conceptual depth. However, any degree of reflection is welcome as it involves students analysing their thinking, their actions and the relationship between these.

Good reflection needs to be taught, and we will look at this in detail below. For now, here are some exemplar reflective questions you can use with your students:

1. How effective was your thinking today? Why?
2. What were you thinking about during the task?
3. What different strategies did you try? Which worked best?

4. If you were going to think about the problem again, what might you do differently?
5. How would you describe your thinking today?
6. If you could go back and give yourself advice on how to think about the problem, what would you say?
7. How do you see your thinking changing next lesson?
8. Which strategies worked? Why did they work?
9. Were you surprised by any of your thinking today? Why?
10. Can you talk me through the different types of thinking you've used today?
11. What impact has your thinking had? How did it help you?
12. What will you take away from today's lesson? How could you use it to change your thinking in the future?
13. How else could you have thought about the problem? What might have been the result?
14. Where did you get stuck today? Why did this happen?
15. What did your mistakes tell you about your thinking?
16. Do you think your thinking was challenged today? Why?
17. If you had to explain your thinking to someone else, how would you do it?
18. Where did you get your ideas from?
19. How did you decide which strategy to use?
20. When was thinking most difficult today? Why?

You can use reflective questioning at various points in the lesson. Plenaries and mid-lesson reviews are obvious examples. However, you can also make it the basis of starter activities (looking back at previous work and then predicting ahead), include it as part of main activities (therefore adding a metacognitive element where otherwise there might have been none), or use it as a standalone tool, for example while you circulate during group work.

**Reflection Training**

We touched on reflection training above. It means training students in how to reflect. This is more important than it might seem. Students won't necessarily be able to reflect in the way you want. And it is very easy to fall into the trap of assuming they know how to reflect automatically.

For example, we might be teaching a lesson, come to the plenary, and then say the following:

'Talk to your partner. Ask them to reflect on what they've learned this lesson and how they think their thinking has changed. Five minutes, then we'll share some ideas.'

Now, there is nothing wrong with this, per se. The intention is clear, the aim is laudable and the design is intended to provoke metacognitive thinking. Yet, there is a glaring ambiguity right at the heart of it all. The word 'reflect'.

Do students know what this means? Do they have a clear understanding of what it entails in practical terms?

Just as we would train students how to decipher command words in preparation for an exam – define, describe, analyse, assess – so we need to ensure they fully understand and can respond to the word 'reflect'.

In our example, we might imagine a pair of students who think they know what reflect means, but don't actually share the same understanding as the teacher. They complete the activity by taking it in turns to list all the things they've done in the lesson, before concluding that they will know all of this when the next lesson comes.

This is not reflection. There isn't a critical engagement here. Nor is there an attempt to reframe what has gone before in relation to any set of criteria.

Effective reflection is best achieved through some prior training. This can take various forms, and you will need to decide what works for you and your students. Here are three examples to get you started:

- Define reflection and 'to reflect' at the start of the year. Display the definition prominently somewhere in your classroom. Take students through a series of simulated reflections in which they practice applying the definition.
- Break reflection down into three parts. For example: 1) Looking at all the thinking you have done, the choices you have made and the results which came about. 2) Decide if your thinking and your

choices led to the results you expected. 3) If they did, examine how you could use this again in the future. If they didn't, look at why and what you could learn.
- Teach students a set of categories they can use as the basis for any reflection. They can look through these categories to identify the things they want to think about. For example, a set of categories for reflecting in A Level Sociology might be: Conceptual understanding; Knowledge of facts and studies; Critical thinking; Evaluation of strengths and weaknesses; Interpretation of information. At Key Stage Four and Five there is scope for using exam mark-schemes as the basis for the categories.

**Cognitive Tools**

Cognitive tools are anything and everything which allow you to broaden the scope of your mind. This broad definition means we could include libraries, the internet and chalk.

Libraries contain a store of information created by minds other than our own, with this information transcending time and space through being captured in books, facilitated by the existence of the alphabet. The internet allows us to access information in a similar manner to the library only with greater scope (in some senses), greater speed and in a wider variety of formats (video and sound as well as text). Chalk allows us to make notes or signs, helping us to remember or keep track of things that we might otherwise forget.

While the definition is broad, the theme is narrow. Cognitive tools help us to go beyond the limits of our own minds. We can think of a subset of these tools being available for classroom use. Here is a list of examples:

- Dictionaries
- Thesauruses
- Crib Sheets
- Formulae Sheets
- Calculators
- Scrap Paper
- Mini-Whiteboards
- Rough Books

- Counting Blocks
- Protractors
- Rulers
- Mnemonics
- Mind-Maps
- Fingers (for counting off a series of items)

In each case, proficiency in using the tool means the student is in a position to do more than they could do without it. This is all about learning how to use tools to solve problems, to think and, ultimately, as strategies.

Take mini-whiteboards as an example. These provide a great space in which students can make mistakes, refine ideas and temporarily store information. Using the mini-whiteboard to do this means the student frees up space in their working memory. This, in turn, means they don't become overloaded, lessening the chance they will withdraw from the work or find the challenge too much.

Training students in how to use different cognitive tools is therefore an excellent way to promote metacognition, particularly if you draw students' attention to what is happening when they use a tool, and why this is to their benefit. You might also want to draw a connection between their use of a tool and the way in which this shapes and changes their thinking. An easy way to do this is to give students a complex problem and ask them to solve it using only their minds. After a few minutes, ask them to use a pencil and some scrap paper as a supporting tool. The difference – physically and mentally – will be immediately obvious.

Finally, it should be noted that different cognitive tools wax and wane in their importance at different times. As a literate adult I find that I only need to use a dictionary occasionally – a student in Year Five may use it rather more often. This also intimates how cognitive tools can be seen through the lens of scaffolding. As the learning to which they give rise becomes embedded, so, in some cases, may use of the scaffold start to decline.

## Narrating Problem-Solving Strategies

Problem-solving strategies are the ways of thinking we employ when faced with challenges. For example, when I am faced with the challenge of writing a book, the first problem-solving strategy I employ is this set of questions:

- What is the topic?
- How can that topic be subdivided into chapters?
- Do I have chapters covering the most important elements of the topic?
- How can I divide each chapter into a series of subsections?
- Does each subsection in each chapter cover something different?
- Are there a sufficient number of practical strategies?
- How should I order the subsections in each chapter?
- How should I order the chapters?

This strategy takes a challenge – writing a book – and breaks it down into a series of separate tasks. It allows me to create a framework for the book which both ensures coverage and provides a set of individual tasks I need to complete to make the book a reality. It also allows me to focus on one thing at a time, safe in the knowledge that there will always be a clear connection to the wider whole (because of the initial work in constructing the framework).

A couple of things follow.

First, we have an example of what a problem-solving strategy looks like. Second, we have an example of what narrating a problem-solving strategy does. It gives the audience – in this case you, the reader – an insight into the thought processes applied in pursuit of a given goal.

Translate this to the classroom and we see that we have a specific example of modelling thinking (see above). Specific because our interest here is solely in narrating, for the benefit of our students, the thought processes we would employ to deal with a specific problem.

Where modelling thinking involves all examples of you giving students access to your expertise, narrating problem-solving strategies is a specific technique in which you talk students through the story of how a strategy works, or how you might apply it if you were them.

Here are some examples of how to use the technique:

- To introduce students to a new way of thinking.
- To help students understand why a particular strategy works.
- To suggest an alternative method to students – which they might then employ, or choose to critique.
- To show students that thinking is malleable and can be changed in light of other people's ideas.
- To illustrate how to deal with a problem in a particular way, with the student going on to copy this or finding an alternative that works for them.
- To provide the basis for student efforts, in that they will take the strategy as a starting point, with this giving them direction where previously there might have been none.
- To give students an insight into how to think about their own thinking. For example, by mimicking the process of narration demonstrated by the teacher.

**Past Work Analysis**

The work that students produce – whether this is written, verbal, physical or material – is the function of the thinking in which they have engaged. Sometimes this thinking is conscious, sometimes not. Sometimes it is of a highly specific nature, sometimes it is fairly general. In some instances, it could be described as instinctual – such as when a footballer strikes a ball, though even this is likely to be the result of prior learning (and, therefore, muscle memory).

Past work analysis means any situation in which students are asked to analyse what they have created or done, in light of the thinking which preceded it – or which can be divined from an examination of the thing in question. It is for this reason that it promotes metacognition.

We are asking students to look back at what they have done. But, instead of seeing the final product as the end point, we ask them to see that as the starting point for an analysis of the processes which led to its formulation. Through this, students are reminded that thinking is open to change, that processes are of central importance, and that they are in a position to shape, edit and refine the thinking they do.

Here are two examples, from different areas of the curriculum, which illustrate the point:

1) Year 5 Science. In the previous lesson, students conducted an experiment. They did this in groups but wrote up their findings individually. The teacher asks students to work in pairs. She encourages them to examine each other's work and to ask questions about this, designed to draw out what the author was thinking at the time.

To help, the teacher first models the process and then displays a set of exemplar questions on the board. She circulates during the activity, prompting and suggesting where necessary. At the end, she leads the class in a shared discussion. This culminates in a set of key points everybody can learn from, concerning how to think scientifically and how to avoid common mistakes.

2) Year 11 Dance. In the previous lesson, students performed pieces they had been developing over a number of weeks. The teacher filmed these pieces and created a set of videos, one per student. Students work in pairs, in a computer room. They look at each of their videos in turn. The teacher then chooses one video, plays it on the main screen and walks students through an exemplar analysis. In this, he focuses on five specific areas, all of which are relevant to the final exam.

As part of this, he is keen to draw attention to any discrepancies between what the student intended and what resulted. His challenge to the class is to analyse how these discrepancies could be dispelled. That is, how greater harmony between thought and action could be achieved. Students then go back to working in pairs. They seek to apply the model the teacher has demonstrated by re-analysing their own work.

**Rehearsing Strategy Selection**

We want students to persist in the face of obstacles. We want them to keep going when things get tough. And we want them to understand that effort is a path to mastery. Specifically, when that effort is targeted in pursuit of a goal.

Rehearsing strategy selection is one metacognitive technique we can use to help achieve this. It works as follows:

Identify a problem students are likely to encounter. This could be a recurring problem such as how to reconcile a design brief with the constraints of materials, time and skills. Or, it could be a one-off problem such as how to measure the area of a non-uniform shape (though, of course, this problem may re-occur in other guises).

Next, think through the obstacles students will encounter when trying to solve this problem. Then, make a note of the possible strategies they could use to overcome these. You now have everything you need: a problem, a set of obstacles connected to that problem, and a collection of strategies for reconciling all of this.

The final step is to plan an activity in which you take students through this, step-by-step. First, you introduce the problem. Then, you talk students through the various obstacles which may arise when trying to solve it. As you do, you can invite students to suggest ways to resolve these. Finally, you start to feed in the strategies you previously identified, on each occasion encouraging students to try them out, play around with them and assess how helpful they are.

Conclude the activity with a review of what happened. Focus students' attention on the relationship between strategy selection and outcome. Ask questions such as:

- Which strategies proved most effective and why?
- How did the different strategies lead you to think differently?
- What impact did the strategies have on how you perceived the task?

This process gives students an extended experience of strategy selection and application to a relevant problem. In so doing, it achieves three things. First, it shows students how to apply strategies to a problem and why this is a good approach to employ. Second, it demonstrates that persistence is key to overcoming obstacles – the rehearsal included the application and analysis of a number of strategies, after all. Third, it reinforces the fact that students are in control of their own thinking, and that this extends to them changing and adapting their thinking to deal with and overcome any problems they face.

**Modelling Self-Regulation**

Our final entry concerning metacognition focuses on the idea of self-regulation. This is the process whereby students exert control over their own actions and thoughts. This control helps them to be more successful. They are able to direct their attention and their focus, perhaps by talking to themselves through an interior monologue, or maybe by switching their approach so as to help themselves keep going.

Here are some examples of self-regulation:

- A student reminds themselves that they need to retain focus when they feel their mind start to wander during a maths lesson.
- A rugby player is about to join a maul when they stop themselves and take up a defensive position based on what the opposition are doing.
- A Year 4 student looks at the clock to see how long they have left to finish their work. They speed up as a result.
- A teacher feels themselves spending too long with a specific group of students. They make a conscious effort to talk to a wider range of pupils.
- A Year 11 student immediately starts writing an essay answer in an exam. They stop themselves, spend thirty seconds thinking up a rough plan, and then continue.

In each example we see the individual taking control of their own behaviour and, through this, giving themselves a better chance of achieving the goal they are working towards.

Self-regulation is a form of metacognition because it involves us being aware of our own thinking, including the limitations which might form part of that thinking, or part of our wider personality (at the present point in time). Armed with this self-knowledge, we are in a position from which to make positive changes should we find ourselves going off-track or doing things in the short-term which run counter to our longer-term goals.

All this leads us to the conclusion that self-regulation is good, that it can be learned, and that students who can do it are going to be in a better position from which to persist and keep going than students who can't do it yet.

For this reason, modelling self-regulation is a great technique to use in the classroom. It sees you demonstrating to students how they can keep a check on their thinking – and what they can do if they find themselves going off-track. Done repeatedly, it helps students develop an understanding of how to regulate their own actions and behaviour. It also draws students' attention to the malleability of their own minds and the potential for growth inherent in all of us.

**Key Points to Take Away**

1) Metacognition means thinking about your own thinking.

2) Doing this means you are in a position to change your thinking.

3) Therefore, metacognition promotes a growth mindset perspective.

4) Giving students access to your expert thinking helps them to develop their own thinking.

5) Metacognitive reflection and analysis helps all students see that their thinking is malleable and open to change.

# Chapter Seven – Creating a Challenge Culture

## Introduction

Students working under the perspective of a growth mindset are more likely to see challenges as a good thing. For them, challenges present an opportunity to learn. There is no conflict between the inevitable difficulties that a challenge throws up and the individual's sense of self. In fact, there is likely to be a fit between the two. This is because the student who adopts an incremental view of intelligence, talent and ability sees the benefit of challenges in helping them to grow and develop.

On the other hand, a student operating under a fixed mindset perspective may well dislike challenges and, possibly, seek to avoid them. This is in large part because challenges are perceived as threatening to the student's sense of self. If, they reason, I have a fixed amount of talent, ability or intelligence, then a challenge which causes me difficulties and risks me failing is likely to show me up for want I can't do. Therefore, it is best avoided.

In the second formulation, the growth benefits of challenge are hard to fathom. This is because the individual is operating from a premise that they possess a fixed sum which cannot be altered. Starting from this premise makes it very difficult to reason cogently that taking on challenges can be beneficial.

Challenge-avoidance can manifest itself in many different ways. More-able students may coast, deliberately, in an attempt to avoid being pushed. Less-able students (at this point in time) may withdraw from tasks or give up quickly, so as to steer clear of the threat of failure they perceive as being contained within the challenge.

Students of every type may decide to consistently take easier options – and, in the process, may cut themselves off from all sorts of possibilities and opportunities – because of this mindset.

In creating a challenge culture we are aiming to do a few things which will help us to develop growth mindsets across the board.

First, we are aiming to make challenge the norm. That is, we are trying to ensure challenge has a central place in all the lessons we teach, and that this is expected, acknowledged and understood. Second, we are aiming to change student perceptions of challenge. We want them to see the benefits of embracing it. And we want them to see that the risks they perceive as being associated with it are not in fact risks at all. Finally, we want to help students understand how they can persist and, ultimately, succeed in the face of challenges. We want to help them develop skills of thinking and acting which they can use to take control of their learning and of the situations in which they find themselves.

These are our goals. The techniques which follow can help us to achieve them.

**Teach Neuroscience**

Teaching students neuroscience means teaching them what we know about how the brain functions. By doing this, we provide them with an accurate understanding of what happens when we learn. This acts as a counterweight to any fixed mindset perceptions of what is and is not possible. It also helps students to understand why challenge can be difficult, uncomfortable and...well, challenging!

Here are three different strategies you might like to employ:

- **Assemblies.** Set up a series of assemblies introducing students to different parts of the brain. For example, you might begin by showing students what neurons are, how they connect together and what happens, in terms of chemical and electrical messages, when we think. Then, you might go on to look at different sections of the brain, such as the limbic system and the pre-frontal cortex. Finally, you could take students on a journey through what happens when we learn – and how challenge leads to new neuronal connections being formed and existing ones being reinforced and developed.
- **Individual Lessons.** Plan a series of individual lessons, either across a week or across a term. Base each lesson around a different theme. For example: What happens when we learn? What happens to our brains when we face a challenge? How does

learning change your brain? Teach these lessons in the same style as you would teach any other. In so doing, you will help to normalise student perceptions about the brain and how it works. They will see this in the context of the wider learning they do.
- **Registration or Tutor Time.** Plan a series of shorter interventions during registration or tutor time. The benefit of this approach is that you can go back to teaching neuroscience again and again over an extended period. This creates a drip-drip effect, regularly feeding students new information about how their brains work and what happens when they learn.

It is important to note that you will have to do a little bit of research to prepare these sessions. The relevant knowledge falls outside the remit of this book. However, a whole host of useful websites and videos are available online, which you can use to help you in your preparations:

1. You can read about some of the science behind Growth Mindsets here - www.mindsetworks.com/webnav/whatismindset.aspx
2. York University have produced a fantastic guide to memory aimed at classroom teachers - www.york.ac.uk/res/wml/Classroom%20guide.pdf
3. You can view a nice animation visualising brain development here - www.youtube.com/watch?v=8Vo-rcVMgbI
4. The Science Museum has a great site showing how your brain works - www.sciencemuseum.org.uk/WhoAmI/FindOutMore/Yourbrain/Howdoesyourbrainwork.aspx
5. As part of that website, you can find out how your brain grows - www.sciencemuseum.org.uk/WhoAmI/FindOutMore/Yourbrain/Howdoesyourbraingrow.aspx
6. Here's an excellent public information initiative giving detailed information about the brain - www.brainfacts.org/
7. And here we have a step-by-step guide to how the brain works - www.ninds.nih.gov/disorders/brain_basics/know_your_brain.htm

8. This simple introduction to brain plasticity includes useful metaphors you can share with your students - faculty.washington.edu/chudler/plast.html

9. Michael Merzenich, a neuroscientist, talks about our developing understanding of brain plasticity in this TED talk - www.ted.com/talks/michael_merzenich_on_the_elastic_brain?language=en

10. Finally, if you work with younger students, you might want to take a look at the growth mindset resources on Class Dojo - www.classdojo.com

Teaching students about neuroscience means helping them to understand how the brain works. This allows them to see that the growth mindset perspective is a more accurate representation of reality than the fixed mindset one. It also gives them a reference point to explain why challenge can be difficult, but why it is so important as well – because of the changes it causes in our brains.

**Learning Goals vs Performance Goals**

Here are two different goals:

- I really want to understand this topic.
- I want to get an A.

Here are another two:

- I want to be able to talk about existentialism and apply it in novel situations.
- I want to get full marks on the existentialism essay.

In both cases, the first goal is a learning goal and the second goal is a performance goal.

Learning goals see the individual focussing on developing their understanding, skill or ability in relation to a certain topic. Performance goals see the individual focussing on an end point, usually quantifiable. In the first case, learning is an end in itself. In the second case, learning becomes a means to an end.

Performance goals are not to be completely chided. But a fixation on them is likely to lead to a loss of appetite for challenge. The reasoning runs as follows:

If you are targeting a performance goal then you are consistently judging your efforts in relation to this. As a consequence, you are likely judge any mistakes or failures which you make more harshly, because these are seen in the light of the performance goal you are trying to meet. It follows that you will lose motivation to challenge yourself. This is because the perceived threat of failure will loom large in your mind. While you may achieve your performance goals, this may not lead to the depth of learning you could have achieved, and it may feel like a relatively painful process.

Learning goals tend to focus on mastery rather than hitting (often arbitrary) performance thresholds. Look again at the two learning goals above. Both are about mastery. Both involve the individual searching for a better understanding. Within this framework, challenge is welcomed. It presents opportunities for the learner to push themselves and to deepen their understanding of the topic.

As you will note, performance goals can be more readily linked to a fixed mindset perspective, whereas learning goals sit closer to a growth mindset perspective.

For this reason, it is worth promoting learning goals to your class. You can do this by setting them for individual students or the class as a whole, and by showing students how to set them for themselves. As part of this process you might also want to downplay performance goals – or illustrate how they can be made subservient to learning goals (in the two examples above, the student who follows the learning goal will probably be better positioned to achieve the performance goal as well).

Finally, don't be afraid to show students the difference between learning and performance goals. Giving your learners a clear insight into the difference – modelling this contrast for them – means helping them to better appreciate how they can take control of their own learning.

## The Language of Challenge

Establishing a language of challenge in your classroom means finding ways in which to communicate to students that challenge is good, that it is to be expected and that it is to be embraced. There are a few ways in which you can do this.

One option is to develop a selection of challenge questions you then use again and again. For example:

- Why do you think that? Where's your evidence?
- How does this fit with what we were saying earlier?
- How would you try to discover if that is true or not?
- What might be the consequences of this?
- What do you predict will happen, based on what you know?

Used regularly, these questions habituate students to expect that their thinking will be challenged, that they will have to fully justify their answers, and that this is part and parcel of gaining mastery.

Another option is take the concept of reframing (see Chapter Two and Chapter Three) and use this to redefine how you and your students talk about challenge. This might lead you to alter common words or phrases:

- 'Challenge' becomes 'Good Challenge'
- 'It's hard' becomes 'It's hard, so I must be developing my brain'
- 'I can't do it' becomes 'You can't do it yet so it must be a challenge! And challenges are good!'

Each reframing changes the student's perspective on challenge, taking it from a negative to a positive.

Another option is to focus your praise on challenge:

- I like the way you embraced the challenges today, Sid. Seeing you keep going when things got tough was great.
- Excellent work on that last challenge today, Sameera. You kept trying different strategies and found one that worked.
- Great level of effort today, class. I ramped up the level of challenge and you all kept persevering and found ways to succeed. Well done.

Or you can make challenge a central feature of your reflection activities:

- What was the biggest challenge you faced today, and how did you overcome it?
- What does it feel like when you are having your thinking challenged?
- How would you explain the strategies you used to overcome the challenge to someone who hadn't been in the room?

**Making Positive Connections between Mistakes and Challenge**

If a student goes through school without making any mistakes, the chances are that they won't have been sufficiently challenged. The flipside of this is that mistakes are the hallmark of challenge. If a student is making them, the work is probably at a level which pushes them to the edge of what they can do.

With that said, a surfeit of mistakes may signal to the teacher that the work is too difficult, but, by and large, if students are making some mistakes then this tends to indicate that the level of challenge is about right.

To promote a culture of challenge – one in which students embrace challenges when they come along – we need to build positive connections in their minds between mistakes and challenge. This is for a couple of reasons.

First, we want to minimise any perception students might have that mistakes are a signal to give up. Remember that if a student is operating under a fixed mindset perspective, they may well feel that the risks attached to making mistakes are so high as to make them best avoided. We want to negate this view.

Second, we want students to see mistakes for what they are: opportunities to learn. In the context of challenge, this means that students see mistakes as opportunities to work out what has gone wrong and, therefore, what could be done differently next time to avoid similar problems developing.

Third, we want students to understand that if they are not making any mistakes then the work is probably too easy for them. In this formulation, an end to mistake-making signals that it is time to move on, or to ask for something more challenging.

You can draw positive connections between mistakes and challenge in a number of ways. These include:

- By praising students for making mistakes and learning from these, and couching this in the context of challenge.
- By circulating during activities and asking students to show you or tell you about any mistakes they have made and what they've learned from these. You can follow up by connecting this learning to the idea of challenge.
- By making clear to students that you expect them to tell you when they cease making any mistakes and, therefore, when they think they might need some harder work.
- By talking about times in your own life when you've faced challenges which have led first to mistakes, then to learning.
- By creating a system through which students can gauge the level of challenge they feel they are working under, based on how many mistakes they are making and how difficult they are finding the work. This gives them a reference point for quantifying challenge – and for asking for more challenging work.

**Modelling Embracing Challenge**

You are a powerful role model for your students. Whether you are aware of it or not, you can be sure that they are constantly observing you – what you do, how you act and what you say. They won't always be consciously aware of this, but it will be going on nonetheless.

As such, what you do and say in relation to challenge can have a big impact. You can set the tone for your class by modelling a growth mindset perspective. Here are some examples of how to do it:

- **Bring in work you did when you were at school.** Talk to students about this. Show them where you faced challenges, the mistakes you made and how you learned from this. Emphasise the fact that your intelligence, ability and talent has grown and developed because of this – and that theirs can as well.

- **Use examples from your own life to illustrate the benefits of embracing challenges.** These could come from your own education, from your professional life, or from hobbies and leisure pursuits such as sport. Whatever you choose, draw students' attention to the fact that anyone can embrace challenge and that perceived costs connected to ideas about failure are just that – perceived rather than real.
- **Model how to think about challenges.** Talk students through the kind of thinking you do when faced with a challenge. This can include any negative thoughts you have or any fixed mindset voices you hear. Show students how you respond to these, put them to one side and embrace challenges regardless.
- **Narrate the experience of embracing challenge, including any negative aspects, and how students can respond to this.** Here we go one step further. Instead of modelling how to think about challenges, narrate what actually happens, emotionally and intellectually, while you are taking on a challenge. A good way to do this is to turn one of your experiences into a story, with the focus being on your interior monologue as you went through it.
- **Create a checklist for embracing challenge and show students how to use this.** This could be a set of steps for students to go through, or a set of questions they could ask themselves when faced with a challenge. Demonstrate the checklist to students and show them how you have used it outside the classroom when looking to embrace a challenge.

## Create a Challenge Wall

Having a challenge wall in your room means having a focal point for the challenge culture you are building – something you and your students can use, refer to and talk about on a regular basis. There is no set formula for creating such a wall. In fact, many options are open to you. Here are three examples of what you might choose to do:

- Designate a wall and leave this blank at the start of the year, except for a title. For example: 'Class 5G's Challenge Wall!' Either at the start of term, or through the course of the year, invite students to come up with the most challenging questions they can think of. Then, use these to fill up your wall. Explain that you want questions on all sorts of different topics, and invite students to write these on pieces of paper they then pin to the wall. As time progresses, plan lots of opportunities for the class to discuss some or all of these questions. Use the wall as a challenging talking point – one you go back to time and again.

- Set aside a space on one of your classroom walls. Cover this in challenges – problems, questions, extension tasks, riddles, puzzles and so forth. These can be subject specific, or they can run the gamut. It's up to you. There are now a couple of options open to you. First, invite students to go the challenge wall and select a challenge whenever they finish their work early. This creates a sense of fun and excitement around the wall and gives students motivation to embrace challenges. Second, set aside lesson time in which you or a student select a challenge from the wall for the whole class to discuss. You can turn this into a regular activity, helping to embed a culture of challenge in your lessons.

- Create a wall display with the title: 'We're Taking On The Challenge!' or something similar. Explain that this area will eventually contain work from every student in the class, but it will only contain work that shows mistakes students have learned from, examples of how students have persisted to get through challenges, and work which has been revised or edited to make it better than it was. Two things flow from this. First, you are making it clear that work goes on display for reasons of process, not end product. Second, this reinforces the idea that challenge is about changing, growing and developing – and that everybody can do this, regardless of their starting point.

## Stingray Questions

In Ancient Greece, so we are told, the philosopher Socrates walked around the city streets of Athens posing difficult questions to the people he met. His aim was to press them on their thinking, to draw out the assumptions and inconsistencies which lay beneath their thought, and, perhaps, to help them think better as a result. To become wiser.

We know about Socrates through the Dialogues of Plato. In these books, Plato, one of Socrates' students, relates philosophical conversations between his mentor and many others. We do not know if Plato's representation of Socrates gives an entirely accurate picture of his thought, or whether it is more accurately seen as a representation of Plato's thinking.

But, what we can say, is that the character of Socrates poses different types of questions. These include, but are not limited to, gadfly, midwife, ignoramus and stingray questions. It is the last of these with which we are concerned here.

Stingray questions pack a jolt. Just like the stingray itself. They shock or surprise students into thinking differently. They challenge students to look at what they thought they knew from a different angle, and to reassess their thinking as a result. Here are some examples of stingray questions:

- What if you had to describe an algorithm as a poem?
- What if the Vietnam War had ended in the first six months?
- What if what you perceive as courage is seen by other people as recklessness?
- What if you could travel on a beam of light?
- What if this is not a question?

The 'what if' question stem is a useful one to use when formulating stingray questions. It is not the only approach you can take, though. Here are some other examples:

- Imagine you had to do it again but without using any adjectives. What would the story be like then?
- Imagine that gravity was half as powerful, what might happen to this room and the things inside it?
- How would the poem sound if it had been written from the perspective of the lark?
- What would need to occur for 1 + 1 not to equal 2?
- How could you tell me that without using words?
- Where does meaning start?
- Is maths a language?
- How do you know that what you know is true?

- If sport involves luck, why do people try so hard?
- When did you start to understand the meaning of this question?

Stingray questions are an opportunity to have a lot of fun! They push students to think in ways they might otherwise have ignored or passed over. For this reason, and as the questions above illustrate, they are challenging.

Regular use of stingray questions helps you to create a culture of challenge in your classroom. They usually require a little bit of preparation time – but once you have a good one you'll be able to use it year after year. Also, when first introducing them you might need to show students how to go about coming up with answers. This means giving them some strategies for deciphering and then responding to questions of this particular type.

**Bloom's Taxonomy**

Ah, that old chestnut! I'm sure you're familiar with Bloom's Taxonomy of Educational Objectives (for more on which, see my book on the topic and my free resource The Bloom Buster). Here's a quick reminder:

The taxonomy was put together in the 1950s. It classifies the cognitive processes students use in school. These are ranked in a hierarchy of mastery, from easiest to hardest. That is, from knowledge to comprehension to application, to analysis, synthesis and, finally, evaluation (although subsequent research suggests the last two could be switched around).

The taxonomy retains relevance today as the processes it delineates, as well as their relationships to one another, remain the same as they were. It is still in widespread use in teaching and assessment. It is frequently used as a framework underpinning exams and tests.

Two other taxonomies were created at the same time – one covering the psycho-motor domain and one dealing with the affective domain. These have not had the same impact, though there is still much to recommend them (for example, if you teach a practical subject, you might like to investigate some of the psycho-motor taxonomies which have been developed since, as they often provide a better framework for underpinning challenge in practical activities).

So, the taxonomy is a hierarchy. As you go up the levels, the degree of challenge increases. Understanding something (comprehension) is more challenging than recalling it (knowledge). Analysing something is more challenging than applying it, and so on.

All of this leads us to the conclusion that the taxonomy is the teacher's friend. It provides a tried and tested basis for structuring activities, lessons and schemes of work in such a way that the level of challenge consistently increases. Using the taxonomy regularly means that you can ensure the work you plan is always challenging.

In addition, you can use the taxonomy to:

- Tailor questioning to individual students, so that it is suitably challenging.
- Create extension tasks.
- Let students create challenging questions or tasks (by opening it up and inviting them to use it).

Finally, it is worth noting that explaining the taxonomy to students will help them to understand where the level of challenge in your lessons comes from. This makes it easier for them to start establishing strategies when faced with tasks or questions of different types.

Oh, one more thing, here is a set of keywords to help you and your students create your challenge culture:

**Knowledge:** Arrange, Define, Describe, List, Match, Memorise, Name, Order, Quote, Recognise, Recall, Repeat, Reproduce, Restate, Retain.

**Comprehension:** Characterise, Classify, Complete, Describe, Discuss, Establish, Explain, Express, Identify, Illustrate, Recognise, Report, Relate, Sort, Translate.

**Application:** Apply, Calculate, Choose, Demonstrate, Dramatize, Employ, Implement, Interpret, Operate, Perform, Practise, Role-Play, Sketch, Solve, Suggest.

**Analysis:** Analyse, Appraise, Categorize, Compare, Contrast, Differentiate, Discriminate, Distinguish, Examine, Experiment, Explore, Investigate, Question, Research, Test.

**Synthesis:** Combine, Compose, Construct, Create, Devise, Design, Formulate, Hypothesise, Integrate, Merge, Organise, Plan, Propose, Synthesise, Unite.

**Evaluation:** Appraise, Argue, Assess, Critique, Defend, Evaluate, Examine, Grade, Inspect, Judge, Justify, Rank, Rate, Review, Value.

### The Zone of Uncertainty

Some years ago I was reading an introduction to the life and work of the philosopher Soren Kierkegaard. For most of the book I found myself in a daze. It was like wading through a marsh with lead in your boots and a sack of coal strapped to your back. Eventually, I reached the end. But it had all been seriously hard work. For a while afterwards I had a set of concepts buzzing around my head which remained infuriatingly difficult to pin down, let alone apply.

This is an example of going into the zone of uncertainty. This is where challenge takes you. It isn't comfortable, but it's a good place to be. Especially if you persist.

When learning something new, something challenging, you cannot necessarily rely on what you already know to get you through. In fact, the new learning may well require you to recalibrate your existing understanding to take account of it. In my Kierkegaard example I found myself deeply uncertain over how to fully comprehend the ideas presented in the book.

After much thinking, further reading, and the advent of time, I got there, just about.

Telling students about the zone of uncertainty means familiarising them with a useful way in which to characterise the experience of being pushed out of your comfort zone. This is helpful because it gives them a means through to articulate that experience – and it provides you and them with a shared language through which to speak. In addition, by giving the term positive connotations you can use it to build a positive view of challenge in students' minds.

Here are some examples of how the concept can be used during classroom discussion:

- 'Right, this is going to be zone of uncertainty time, so get ready to do some serious thinking!'
- 'If you're finding this difficult – good! It's meant to be a challenge. We're in the zone of uncertainty at the moment, but if we keep working at it we'll pull ourselves out.'
- 'Zone of uncertainty coming up soon, class. Get ready!'
- 'Miss, I think I'm in the zone of uncertainty at the moment – can we discuss this so I can change my thinking on it?'
- 'Sir, I'm definitely right in the middle of the zone of uncertainty with this. But I'm going to keep trying before I ask you for help.'

Idealised examples, perhaps. But they illustrate the benefit of giving a name to the experience of having your thinking challenged. Of course, other names can be used. One common alternative is that of 'the learning pit'. If you search this on Google Images you can get some good pictures to use with your class.

One final point to conclude the chapter. You might like to attach a scale to the zone of uncertainty. For example: 1 – 10. This means you can ask students the question: 'Where are you in the zone of uncertainty at the moment, if 1 is really uncertain and 10 is almost out the other side?'

This option makes it easier for students to define precisely how uncertain they feel, giving you access to more specific information, and helping them to articulate a sense of change as they make progress (for example: 'I was at one, sir, but now I'm like a seven at least!')

**Key Points to Take Away**

1) Students may perceive challenge as having risks attached, causing them to avoid it.

2) Establishing a challenge culture means normalising challenge in your classroom.

3) Building positive associations around challenge helps to change how students think about it.

4) Changing how you and your students talk about challenge is a good place to start.

5) Planning for challenge means ensuring students are always having their thinking pushed.

# Chapter Eight – Focussing on Processes

## Introduction

Imagine someone is baking a cake. After a couple of hours, an end product appears. It sits on a plate, resting on the worktop. Smooth, white icing covers two layers of sponge. Jam is spread between. The cake is decorated with marzipan shapes of different colours. It looks beautiful.

But what has caused the cake to be? What has turned a set of ingredients into an end product? What constitutes the history of the cake's creation?

Process.

When we meet the cake as an end product we find it fixed. Finalised. And this fact can easily give rise to the misnomer that the end product is therefore a result of some fixed or innate qualities existing within the creator of the cake. So, we might say, the cake is as good as it is because the cake-maker is a genius. Or because they're brilliant.

This could be seen to imply that the cake-maker has innate talent which causes them to create enviable cakes. It may also imply that this talent is something the cake-maker is lucky to possess, not something they have striven to develop. In addition, it sets up a deficit position: those who do not have the innate skill of the master cake-maker will never be able to produce cakes such as the one we see before us.

Imagine, though, if an expert baker entered the room and started to look at the cake. Through what eyes would they see the product?

Through the eyes of someone who has experienced the process of cake making time and again. Who, through this process, has come to understand the separate elements which constitute successful execution of the necessary skills. Who appreciates the nuanced range of quality which can result from subtle tweaks or mistakes that may be made in each of those elements.

If we look at end products as being without history, we risk focussing our attention on traits and innate qualities, seemingly suggesting that these are the causes of what we see.

If, however, we acknowledge that all products are the end result of prior work, then we begin to turn our attention to the effort and the other processes which have led to their creation. Effort can be targeted, changed and developed. Processes can be improved, learned and reflected on. We thus find ourselves in a position from where we can talk about growth much more easily.

Instead of risking the possibility that we discuss and respond to an end product as a fixed entity, we find ourselves ready to discuss such a product as the result of processes – as being achieved incrementally, through the accumulation of effort in given directions.

This leads us to three conclusions. Conclusions which underpin the practical strategies in this chapter:

1. All students can improve, change and adapt the processes they use to think, work and create things.
2. Drawing attention to processes means getting students to think about what they have done, what has resulted and how changes to the former can lead to changes in the latter.
3. Focussing on processes promotes growth mindsets and sends a clear message that everybody can develop their talent, ability and intelligence.

**Processes of Learning versus Goals of Performance**

In Chapter Seven we looked at the difference between learning goals and performance goals. We said that emphasis on the former is a good way to promote growth mindset thinking. Here, we can look at this in the context of processes.

If I am obsessed with scoring a try in a rugby match, all I will think about is scoring a try. Every time I see the ball coming towards me, I will set myself with the intention of scoring. Sometimes I will, and sometimes I won't. When I do, I will be delighted that I have done what I wanted to do. When

I don't, I will feel I have failed, at least in comparison to the goal I set myself.

If I am focussed on the processes which give rise to try-scoring opportunities, things might be different. Every time I see the ball coming towards me, I will think about the things I need to do to give myself the best chance of scoring. My focus will be on executing the processes and observing what is in front of me. When I score, I will reflect on how my actions helped me to do this. When I don't score, I will analyse why – and ask myself what I can learn from the attempt. What I might do differently next time.

This idealised vignette demonstrates the difference between having a dominant focus on performance and a dominant focus on learning. The former often creates a zero-sum game of success or failure in the mind of the thinker. In addition, it leaves little room for the benefits of reflective analysis and concomitant development.

The latter promotes a focus on processes because these are perceived as part of the path to mastery. Get the basics right, and the rest will follow. Refine the basics, improve and develop them, and even more becomes possible.

When helping students in your class to think about and reflect on the processes they use in lessons, this is what we are aiming to achieve. Not an outright dismissal of performance goals (after all, the later example above still has an ultimate result of wanting to score a try), but a dominant position for learning goals.

For this reason, it is worth talking to students about the differences between the two types of goals. It is also worth explaining why you talk about processes, give feedback on processes and draw students' attention to this. All the while, you will be helping them appreciate the benefits of seeing their intelligence, talent and ability as open to change. As intimately tied up with the processes in which they engage. Processes they can develop.

## Defining Process

One of the problems with talking about processes is that the term can be vague or ambiguous. So what do we mean when we use it? And how can we convey this meaning to our students?

Put simply, a process is a procedure we go through in order to do or produce something. We might use a series of processes when creating a piece of work, or we might practice using just one, depending what is at issue. Here are some examples of processes:

-   **A student is writing an essay.** Processes include: sequencing ideas; applying a paragraph structure; following success criteria; making revisions; using the conclusion to give an opinion.
-   **A student is practising a dance routine.** Processes include: thinking about the routine; observing what happens on each attempt; making tweaks and changes; focussing on specific sections of the routine; paying attention to transitions; seeking and using feedback.
-   **A student is conducting a science experiment.** Processes include: collecting and checking data; paying attention to detail; controlling variables; observing what happens; making judgements about the data collected.
-   **A teacher is planning a lesson.** Processes include: delineating the topic; thinking about what the class already know; deciding on the structure of the lesson; picking out activities; refining the questions that need to be answered; fitting the content into the structure.
-   **A student is learning a new topic.** Processes include: paying attention; focussing effort; making connections with what is already known; trying different problem-solving strategies; asking for and implementing feedback; analysing information.

We need to make a few points here, before we go on.

First, the examples above are not exhaustive. They serve only to demonstrate what we mean by processes and the range of processes which might be used in different situations. Second, there are two wider processes contained in all of the examples above: the process of learning and the process of thinking.

Third, one of the common criticisms of focussing on processes is that it denigrates knowledge and overemphasises skills. While it can be seen why this charge might be made, it is not a reasonable one to bring.

Processes are always used in context. So, for example, the student who is writing the essay is writing that essay about something. Therefore, the processes on which they call are used in the context of the knowledge and understanding they have developed. Equally, the teacher who is planning a lesson uses the processes outlined above to apply their knowledge and understanding, both of the lesson content and of pedagogy more broadly.

Thus, while we might define process as the procedures we use to do things, these procedures do not exist independently of knowledge – they cannot. They are always used in conjunction with knowledge.

So, when we give students feedback on processes, or draw their attention to these, in order to foster learning goals and a growth mindset perspective, we do so with the intention that students will implement this in the context of some knowledge – that they possess already, or that they will learn as a consequence of our lessons.

**Modelling, Suggesting, Prompting and Clueing**

We can help students to think about and refine the processes they use during the course of any lesson. Four good ways to do this are modelling, suggesting, prompting and clueing. Here are some examples of how each one works:

**Modelling:** We can model processes for students in many different ways. For example, we might show them how to think about a particular type of mathematical problem, and then encourage them to copy this and see how it works. Or, we might show them how to edit a sentence using a three step method, such as: Does it make sense? Could I say the same thing in fewer words? Does it fit with the rest of the paragraph? Another option is to continuously model a growth mindset approach to thinking and learning. Doing this gives students a model of how to engage with the lesson content premised on the idea that intelligence, talent and ability are open to change. This is like a meta-process. A way of looking at learning which underpins and influences everything else.

**Suggesting:** We can suggest to students how they might tweak or change a process they are using in an effort to achieve something. For example, a PE teacher might observe a student shooting for the basket in netball while not keeping their head still. They might step in and say: 'Mary, as you go to shoot, focus your attention on your head. Hold it still, line up the shot and then shoot.' Another option is to suggest alternative processes which students might try. For example, a science teacher observing a group of students trying to solve a problem might step in and suggest a different problem-solving strategy.

**Prompting:** A prompt is a little less invasive than a suggestion. It places slightly more onus on the student. We can prompt students by asking questions or by reminding them of things they might have forgotten or overlooked. Here are some examples:

'Steve, how do we keep our balance when running with the ball?'

'Tiana, are there any different approaches you know of that might be worth trying?

'Ahmed, what happened when you tried to do it that way last time? What could you do instead?

In each of these cases we are prompting students to think about the processes in which they are engaged. It is akin to reminding students of the benefits of analysing their own thinking. Which, as we know, is often a feature of growth mindset thinking.

**Clueing:** This sees us giving students clues which can help them to change, adapt or reflect on the processes in which they are engaged. It is not too dissimilar to prompting, if slightly more opaque, and once again puts the onus on students. Here are some examples:

'Trial and error might be something to think about here, Paul.'

'I wonder if the success criteria could help you to develop what you're doing, Rebecca?'

'If it's not working, what could you change?'

'Rima, is there something in the instructions which could help?'

'Kyran, is there a strategy from last lesson that might work?'

**Process Feedback: Lists and Implementation**

We looked at feedback in depth in Chapter Five. Here, I want to show you two techniques you can use to focus your feedback on processes and to maximise the impact of that feedback. First, process lists.

Here is a (non-exhaustive) process list from GCSE Sociology:

- Break questions down into separate parts.
- Look at issues from more than one point of view.
- Compare different pieces of evidence to see if they agree.
- Weigh up the strengths and weaknesses of sociological ideas.
- Use sociological terminology when writing about sociology.
- Think critically – question the ideas you hear and read.
- Use evidence and examples to support any points you make.
- Compare what you experience in society to what sociologists have said and discovered.
- Avoid 'common sense' explanations and focus on sociological ones.
- Make connections between current events and what we study.

And here is a (non-exhaustive) general processes list:

- Use trial and error to improve your work.
- Try different strategies to solve problems.
- Focus your attention on the task in hand.
- Ask for feedback when you feel you need it.
- Remind yourself to stay on task.
- Improve and refine your work as you go.
- Examine how effective your thinking is.
- Check your work before handing it in.
- Compare your work with the success criteria.
- Break difficult tasks down into smaller, simpler tasks.

Imagine you were now about to sit down to mark a pile of books. These lists provide you with a fantastic reference point. You can use them as the basis of your feedback. Instead of having to think from scratch every time you come to write a comment, you can refer to the lists, select a process relevant to the student in question, and frame your feedback around this.

Delineating subject-specific and general processes in this way makes formative feedback quicker and easier. It also helps you to keep your focus on processes and allows you to identify in advance what you would like students in your class to be working towards.

Finally, there is the added benefit that you can share these process lists with your students. They can then use them as a basis for regulating their own learning, developing their thinking and reflecting on the progress they are currently making.

We now move onto our second point: implementation.

While focussing feedback on processes is to be welcomed, the efficacy of this feedback will diminish considerably if students are not given dedicated time in which to implement it. Without this time, there is a strong likelihood that the feedback will disappear into the ether – even if teacher and student both start out with the best of intentions.

As we saw in Chapter Five, there are many ways you can help students to implement your feedback. But they all share a common theme: specific time is set aside in which everybody's focus is on feedback implementation. One example will serve to reinforce the point.

A learner driver reaches the end of their lesson. The driving instructor talks them through what they did well and what they could improve. The feedback focuses on processes. It concludes with a target: 'Next week,' says the instructor, 'I would like you to pay attention to finding the bite when you lift the clutch. Try to feel in your legs the change in pressure – and listen for the noises which come alongside it as well.'

In scenario one, next week's lesson begins with thirty minutes clutch control practice, first in a car park, the on a housing estate and finally on a set of quiet 'A' roads.

In scenario two, next week's lesson makes no mention of the feedback and no time is given to practising clutch control.

And that is why dedicated target implementation time matters. Students need to be able to focus their attention on one thing, to practice this, and, if necessary, to receive further feedback as they do. That is how change happens.

**Discussing Learning Mid-Flow**

We now turn our attention to a different approach. One which sees processes being examined during the course of activities.

Discussing learning mid-flow means either engaging students in a conversation about what they are doing, while they are doing it, or facilitating a similar conversation between peers. The aim is to help students attend to the processes they are using. Those things which make up the thinking and learning they are doing. (Here you can see the link to metacognition.)

Let us look at both techniques in turn.

While students are taking part in an activity, circulate through the room. Observe what is happening, examine the work students are producing, and listen to any conversations which are going on. Identify which students you would like to intervene with.

Step in and begin a conversation with one of these students. Ask them about what they are doing. Depending on their response, either move the discussion onto processes straight away, or take it there gradually. Here is an example:

**Teacher:** How are you getting on with the problems?

**Student:** Yeah, not too bad, sir. I've done the first few.

**Teacher:** How did you try to solve them?

**Student:** Well I used that technique you showed us last lesson. It was pretty easy to apply.

**Teacher:** What made it easy?

**Student:** There wasn't much different between the questions and the example you showed us, so I didn't have to change a lot.

**Teacher:** What about this question? Do you think you might have to change the technique?

**Student:** Hmmm, maybe, yeah. It looks a bit different.

**Teacher:** What makes it different from the other questions?

Here we see the teacher encouraging the student to think about the problem-solving technique they've used, both in relation to the past and as regards the future. The conversation helps the student attend to the problem-solving process in a way they might otherwise have missed. The teacher could go on to make more explicit links to growth mindset thinking, or simply leave this implicit.

You can also facilitate student discussion of learning mid-flow. The easiest way to do this is to stop the class mid-way through an activity, draw students' attention to some key processes they are using, and then pose one or two questions for them to discuss in pairs. For example:

**Teacher:** 'OK, everybody, eyes on me for a minute. Now, we've been using Freud's theory to try to explain aggression. But how effectively have you been comparing his theory with the different examples of aggressive behaviour? Talk to your partner and ask them to assess how accurate and precise they've been in applying Freud's theory. Then ask them to tell you how they've been identifying the areas where it doesn't seem to fit.

These instructions ask students to look critically at the thinking they are doing. Specifically, they ask them to focus on the process of application and the process of identifying discrepancies. These are general thinking skills important in the study of psychology. In the example they are contextualised in light of specific knowledge (Freud's theory).

You can call on this technique in almost any activity you ask students to complete. However, it becomes more effective with repetition, if you train students in how to do it, and if you explain the purpose behind it (which gives it greater meaning in students' eyes).

## Process Questions

Implicit in much of what we have said so far is the fact that you can always ask students questions about the processes they are using to learn and to think. Chapter Ten provides a list of 25 exemplar questions of this type. Here are five ways you can use such questions:

- **As the basis of mid-lesson reviews and plenary activities.** This is fairly obvious. The questions promote metacognition and encourage students to reflect on what they are doing, why they are doing it, and what is happening as a result. The fit with mid-lesson reviews and plenaries is a natural one. In either case, repeated use habituates students into thinking in this way.
- **By creating a process-checklist for students to use independently.** Identify five process questions relevant to your teaching and turn these into a checklist students can use to monitor and improve the thinking and learning they do. You might decide to have a general checklist which retains relevance across the board, or you might choose to create a series of separate checklists for different topics or activity types.
- **By creating a bag of questions from which and your students can pick at random.** Type up the process questions in Chapter Ten, print these out, cut them up and place the resulting pieces of a paper in an opaque bag. You now have a random selection tool! During activities or at the end of the lesson, bring the bag out and invite a student to select a random process question. Pose this question to the whole class and then facilitate a debate.
- **As the basis of lesson or task success criteria.** Students use success criteria to direct their efforts during an activity, or across a lesson as a whole. Keep their focus on processes by using process questions as the basis of your success criteria. For example, instead of giving students three statements as success criteria, you might give them three process questions. They then have to keep checking whether they can answer these successfully as they go through the task. When they can, they know they have been successful. When they can't yet, they know how they need to target their efforts (or what to target their efforts towards).

- **As a tool through which students can self-assess.** Provide students with a list of process questions – such as the one in Chapter Ten – and encourage them to use this as a self-assessment tool through the course of the year. Explain that students should choose two or three questions from the list and use these to assess their work as they go. Indicate the benefits they are likely to draw in terms of self-regulation, metacognition and improving the quality of their thinking and learning.

## Analysing and Reflecting on Strategies

Students working under a growth mindset perspective are more likely to keep going when things get challenging. As part of this, they will deploy different strategies in an effort to find out what works. They will also analyse and reflect on the results of their efforts. This leads them to develop their understanding of how to succeed in a given task or with a given topic.

We can help all students to develop a growth mindset by setting up opportunities in which everyone can analyse and reflect on the strategies they have used. In addition, we can give students access to the thinking of their peers, allowing them to see and hear what strategy analysis and reflection looks and sounds like.

Here are five examples of how to do it:

- **Strategy Collation.** At the end of an activity or towards the end of a lesson, ask students to share the different strategies they have been using. Collate these on the board. Then, ask students to get into groups of two or three. Assign each group one of the strategies. Their task is to analyse this. It may include going and speaking to the person who shared it. They need to be ready to report back to the class about how the strategy works, when it might be useful and whether it could be adapted.
- **Reflection Sheets.** Create a reflection sheet which students can use to analyse and reflect on the strategies they employ during a lesson, activity or topic. This is essentially a reflection pro-forma with an emphasis on problem-solving strategies. Students can note down what strategy they used, when they used it, why they

used, how effective it was, and how they could adapt it in the future. Develop by having students interview their peers and adding the reflections they hear to their own sheets, perhaps in a different colour.

-   **Write me a letter.** Ask students to write you a letter explaining, analysing and reflecting on the strategies they used in a particular task. Provide relevant guidance and use modelling and scaffolding where necessary. Read the letters students write when you take in their work – this will give you a good insight into who is thinking effectively about processes and who needs more support. Simplify by asking students to write a short paragraph (perhaps on an exit pass) instead of a letter.

-   **Peer-Tutoring.** Identify the students who are most able to analyse and reflect on the strategies they use to solve problems, think and learn. Charge these students with the task of tutoring their peers. Divide the class into groups, ensuring one of the identified students is in each group, and give these students time in which to talk their peers through the strategies they have been using, how they have been using them, and whether they have been effective or not.

-   **Peer-Modelling.** Identify one or two students skilled in analysing and reflecting on the strategies they use to solve problems. Use their thinking as a model for the rest of the class. Talk through what they have been doing and, if appropriate, show what the results of this have been. Ask students to discuss what you have shown them with a partner and to identify what they could borrow, adapt or copy from their peer's model.

## Key Points to Take Away

1) Processes are what we use to think, learn, problem solve and create things.

2) Focussing on processes means looking at the things we do and thinking about how we could change or adapt these.

3) Processes do not exist independently of knowledge and understanding.

4) Helping students to think about processes means cultivating growth mindset traits.

5) There is important overlap between focussing on processes and thinking about thinking.

# Chapter Nine – Engaging Parents with Growth Mindsets

## Introduction

If students are hearing the same growth mindset messages at home as they are hearing at school, then there is a higher likelihood they will internalise those messages. Engaging parents with growth mindsets is therefore a two-step process. First comes communication. Second is providing tools and techniques. We'll look at each in turn.

Many parents will never have heard of growth mindsets, Carol Dweck or the body of work she has produced. The first step is to change this. Communicating to parents about growth mindsets means giving them an insight into the research you are using to inform teaching and learning in your school. It also means opening up that teaching and learning, along with any other aspects of school life, to show parents what the theory means in practice.

Approaching parental engagement in this way means setting yourself three clear goals to achieve before moving onto tools and techniques:

1) Ensuring every parent knows what growth mindsets are and what Dweck's research suggests.
2) Telling parents why growth mindsets is important, what benefits it can bring to their children, and why this is better than the status quo.
3) Showing parents what change looks like in the classroom, in the wider school and in students' thinking and learning.

Each step builds on the one before. Once parents know what growth mindsets are, they are ready to be convinced of the benefits. Once they are convinced of (or, at least, have heard) the benefits, they are ready to know more about what the school is doing.

At this point, there is a natural segue into step two.

Hopefully, parents will be convinced of the benefits and supportive of the changes the school is making. They will then ask: but what can I do? And this is where you present them with the tools and techniques they can use at home to support their children.

The process of engaging parents is thus partly about getting them to a point where they are ready to receive ideas they can put into practice. If the groundwork isn't done first, sharing the tools and techniques may prove a fruitless exercise. We need to sell the efficacy of promoting growth mindsets before showing parents how to go about doing it.

In the rest of this chapter we'll look at practical measures connected to both these steps. The next five entries deal with step one – communication – while the last four cover tools and techniques.

**Information Evenings**

Information evenings are a simple way through which to tell parents about growth mindsets. You can run a single event, a series of linked events, or a series of repeat sessions. Whichever option you choose, the aim is the same: to give parents an insight into Dweck's research, growth mindset theory and the consequences for learning, thinking and how children perceive themselves.

A key obstacle is ensuring parental attendance. Here are five strategies you can use to boost numbers and to reach as many parents as possible:

- **Scheduling.** Think carefully about the scheduling of any event. Ask yourself what will make life easiest for parents in your area. For example, could you provide a crèche service or a film room for the duration of the event? Another possibility is to present parents with a choice of three options for when an information evening could be scheduled, and to then go with the date that receives the most support.
- **Broadcast the information evening.** If you film the information evening you can publish it online – either through YouTube or via your school website. Doing this means you can reach parents who do not attend. It also gives you the option of reminding parents, in person or via email, to review the film – keeping growth mindsets at the top of their agenda.
- **Create supplementary materials.** For example, a booklet. You can give this to parents who attend the evening but you can also

email a PDF version to all parents who don't attend. This is another way of reaching those parents and of giving them a way to access the content.

- **Use social media.** The various social media platforms provide a great way through which to engage parents and to build interest in an event. An added benefit is that you can share some of the growth mindsets content already available online – such as videos, articles and interviews with Carol Dweck. This helps prime parents to attend your event and also demonstrates that growth mindsets is a well-supported idea with a high level of cachet.
- **Invite a guest speaker.** Doing this can increase the number of attendees due to the novelty value or because of the reputation of the speaker. Options include teaching and learning experts, teachers from schools in your area who are further on in their mindset journeys, psychologists from local universities, or individuals who have used growth mindset theory to achieve something – such as a local sportsperson.

**Parents' Evening Opportunities**

Parents' evenings are another fantastic opportunity for communicating about growth mindsets. The traditional high turnout means it is a chance to reach a large number of parents. More, perhaps, than might attend an information evening. In addition, parents will be thinking about their child's learning and will be ready to ask questions such as: What can we do to help? If you're lucky, this can make looking at growth mindsets on parents' evenings like shooting into an open goal.

Here are five ways to take advantage of the opportunity:

- **Information Booklets.** Create an information booklet to hand out to parents covering all the key information they need to know about growth mindsets. You might also like to include an overview of what the school is doing (and why it is doing it) to promote the idea.
- **Headteacher's Talk.** Schedule a talk by the headteacher and invite parents to attend while they are at the parents' evening. In this talk, the head should communicate to parents what growth

mindset theory is and why it matters to them, their school and their students.

- **Work Displays.** Create a display of student work with an explicit growth mindset theme. For example, you could have a display called: Good Mistakes and What They Teach You. Or, one called: What can we learn through trial and improvement? This provides a talking point, giving you and your colleagues a way to engage parents with growth mindsets. You might like to create a booklet or leaflet to go alongside the display that parents can take away with them.
- **Growth Mindset Student Film.** Create a student film in which growth mindset messages are to the fore. You can play this for parents in a series of showings, or have it playing on a loop somewhere near the entrance, for parents to watch when they first arrive.
- **Teacher Messages.** Ask colleagues to help you get the growth mindset message across to parents by including key mindset themes in their conversations. For example, you might ask colleagues to explain why making mistakes is a good thing and what they are doing to minimise students' fear of failure.

A final point to note is that you can use parents' evenings to find out what parents already know about growth mindsets, or what their perceptions of learning are. The easiest way to do this is through a survey or questionnaire handed out at the entrance to the event.

**Changes to Reporting**

Reports are one of the main ways schools interact with parents. Changing the make-up of your reports gives you another way to communicate growth mindset ideas. Here are five examples of what you can do:

- **Growth Mindset Preamble.** Write a growth mindset preamble to put at the front of every report you send to parents. In this you can set out the aims of the school in terms of growth mindsets. What you are trying to do and how you think this will help your students. This is like having a growth mindset mission statement at the start of each report. The only caveat is that you must ensure the messages contained in the preamble are echoed by the content of the teacher comments which follow.

- **Focus on Challenges.** Make embracing challenge a central feature of your reports. In a primary school, this might involve the class teacher highlighting how each student has embraced challenge through the term or the year. In a secondary school, this might see each subject teacher setting a challenge for the student to embrace in the coming months.

- **Report on Effort.** If effort is the path to mastery than it needs to be front and centre at all times. Include a section in your reports where the focus is exclusively on effort. Give this value and authority by placing it above any summative grades. Ask teachers to talk in terms of effort when writing reports and to consistently make the connection between the effort a student puts in and the progress they achieve as a result.

- **Give teachers growth mindset vocabulary to use.** Provide teachers with a set of growth mindset words and phrases they can use while writing their reports. This crib sheet will keep growth mindset ideas at the front of their minds. It also gives you a way to create consistency of language across a wide range of reports. This is particularly valuable in a secondary school, where a parent might receive reports written by ten or eleven different teachers.

- **Set learning goals, not performance goals.** Learning goals focus on development of knowledge and understanding whereas performance goals aim for a finite end. You could set both, or you could just set learning goals. If the latter, make clear to parents why this is happening and also ensure that teachers keep the goals precise and specific to avoid accusations of vagueness or ambiguity.

## Talking in Terms of Character

One of the reasons so many teachers are interested in growth mindsets is because it is about educating the whole child. Development of character is wrapped up in the approach, just as much as raising achievement and finding ways to maximise student progress.

Talking in terms of character fits easily with any attempt you make to introduce growth mindsets to your classroom or your school. We can talk in terms of character to parents as well. But what benefits can this bring?

The first, I would argue, is that character is a term many parents will find it easy to empathise with. While they might not have much background knowledge of psychology, learning theory or pedagogy, they will definitely know what character is and, quite possibly, have their own views on what it means to teach character to a young person.

Connecting growth mindsets to the development of character thus gives you another way to communicate with parents. One which might allow you to reach some who would otherwise be difficult to engage.

Here are three examples of what you can do:

- **The Characteristics of a Successful Learner.** In conjunction with colleagues, define what characterises a successful learner in your school. Connect this to growth mindsets and create an overview you can share with parents, students and staff. Use this as the basis for talking about learning, as a tool through which to plan student development, and as a framework for writing reports and communicating with parents more generally.
- **Praise and Celebrate Character.** For example, through assemblies, through letters home, or through reports. In each case, draw attention to the character traits displayed by the students in question. Link these to growth mindsets and draw a connection between the decisions students make, the effort they put in and the outcomes which result.
- **Character Newsletter.** Start a regular character newsletter to send to parents. This could be termly or more frequent, depending on your circumstances. Use the newsletter to communicate about the character traits of successful learners, how this links to growth mindsets, and to celebrate examples of resilience, determination, and effort shown by students inside and outside school.

## Consistency of Messages

Our final entry covering part one – communication – concerns the consistency of the messages parents hear from you, your colleagues and the school as a corporate entity (such as via newsletters and through the website).

A message will always be more powerful if it is clear and succinct. This is particularly important when that message is first being conveyed. If parents hear different messages, they will be confused. This confusion may extend to their understanding of growth mindsets. Or, they may simply be confused about why the school is sending out mixed signals.

To create and ensure a consistent message, there are a few things you need to think about.

First, a degree of prior work needs to be done. This covers clarification, refinement and synthesis of your thinking about growth mindsets. Only once you have been through this will you be in a position to pare down your message to its basic elements. To illustrate, consider the difference between these two messages:

- Our school is on a growth mindsets journey. We want every student to start thinking positively about mistakes, to try things out, to take risks, and not to be afraid of getting things wrong if it helps them to learn.
- We want all students to see mistakes as opportunities to learn.

For me, the second message is preferable. Sure, the first message could form part of your communication later on. But the second one is succinct and precise. It is easier to remember, easier to communicate. The work has been done in advance. The result is crisper, cleaner, leaner.

Second, with your messages defined, you need to ensure that all staff buy into these and are happy to use them as part of their communication with parents. Perhaps the biggest hurdle here is getting over any resistance to the idea that messages are being imposed from on high. The best way to counter this is through reference to the common good. Individual liberty is being slightly eroded, but this is so that all parents receive the same messages about growth mindsets. Which, ultimately, should benefit every student in the school.

Third, and finally, you may need to look at some of your existing communication with parents and assess whether it fits with the mindset messages you have defined. For example, if you send postcards home praising students for being clever or achieving perfect scores, then these will need to be amended as they run counter to the growth mindset tenets you are trying to promote.

## Exemplar Questions

We move now to the second part of engaging parents – providing them with tools and techniques they can use to support their children at home.

Here is a set of twenty-five exemplar questions designed for parents. You can share these as they are, or amend them to fit your context. Either way, they provide a fantastic starting point for discussions and conversations which have a growth mindset focus.

1. Can you show me what great effort looks like?
2. How does effort help you to learn?
3. When you're putting in effort, how do you keep yourself on track?
4. Why does effort help you to change what you can do?
5. Is it good to keep going, even if things get tough? Why?
6. Can you tell me about the best mistake you made at school today?
7. What makes a good mistake?
8. What did you learn from your mistakes this week?
9. Are some mistakes better than others, why?
10. That's an interesting mistake, what do you think about it?
11. What an interesting picture – what made you choose those colours?
12. I like what you've done here – can you tell me more about it?
13. What made you decide to do it that way?
14. This is interesting – what were you thinking about when you did it?
15. How could I get better at learning? What would you suggest to me?

16. What's the best way to keep going when things get tough?
17. If you're learning something difficult, what can you do to keep going?
18. Can you tell me about the different thinking you've done at school today?
19. What makes good thinking?
20. What was the best challenge you faced today?
21. What do you like about having your thinking challenged?
22. What makes a problem really interesting?
23. Can you tell me how you improved this before you finished it?
24. Is it good to keep trying different strategies when you get stuck? Why?
25. Can you change your intelligence? How?

When you share these questions – or your own ones – it's useful to include a couple of examples of the kind of conversations to which they might give rise. This provides a model parents can use to get started. The exemplification points them in the right direction and can reassure them if they feel uncertain about whether what they are doing is right or not.

**Exemplar Language Changes**

Another technique you can show parents is how to modify their language so as to avoid fixed mindset messages and encourage growth mindset ones. This takes its cue from the idea of reframing. Something we have examined elsewhere in the book.

The idea is to give parents a set of exemplar language changes they can implement in their own speech – rather than asking them to reframe the language their children use. This latter idea may be suitable for them further down the line, but is probably a little too demanding initially, while they are still getting to grips with growth mindset ideas.

Here is a set of exemplar language changes we could give to parents as a starting point:

- That's brilliant, **becomes:** That's interesting, what made you think in that way?
- You're a genius, **becomes:** Tell me about it – how did you decide what to do?

- Don't worry, I couldn't do it either, **becomes:** I'm sure if we look at it together we can work out a solution.
- That's too hard, **becomes:** Challenges are good because you know you're brain's having to work hard.
- We're not that type of family, **becomes:** If you keep trying I think you'll be able to do it.

You can use this set of language changes or come up with your own. Either way, the aim is to both provide parents with a starting point for changing some of the things they say, and to exemplify the difference between fixed mindset and growth mindset thinking through the contrasting language.

Another option is to give parents a set of exemplar changes which reflect the linguistic currency you are developing in school. This sees you sharing how certain terms have been rebranded, with the intention that parents will buy into this and echo the changes when talking with their child. Here is an example:

- Mistakes, **become:** Good mistakes
- Trial and error, **becomes:** Trial and improvement
- Difficult, **becomes:** Our next challenge
- I can't, **becomes:** I can't yet
- I can't do it, **becomes:** What strategy could I try next?

Whichever option you go for, it can be helpful to provide parents with a print-out or sticker they can place somewhere prominent in their home (such as on the fridge door) to act as cue. You can distribute this in person, via email or send it home with students.

**Three Parenting Tools**

In our final two entries we will look at six parenting tools adapted from ideas found elsewhere in this book. All have been simplified. All can be taught to or shared with parents at information evenings, via newsletters, or through other means appropriate to your school.

- **Mental Contrasting.** If...then... **If** I want to improve my science project, **then** I will need to edit my work and check my data. Showing parents the technique of mental contrasting means giving them a simple tool to which they can turn when they want to help their child achieve a goal. They simply need to rephrase what the child has said into the form of 'If...then...' They will also be able to use the technique at other times, for example, to pre-empt something their child might be getting ready to say. Or, to change the focus of a conversation from negative to positive.

- **Story-Telling.** You can teach parents the importance of paying attention to the stories they and their children tell about themselves. As part of this, demonstrate how certain stories can reinforce a perception of yourself as a learner in which intelligence, talent and ability are fixed. Highlight the fact that these stories can easily bubble up to the surface without us even realising – and that we need to be alive to them if we want to avoid them, rephrase them or tell different stories altogether. You might also want to give parents of younger children a list of growth mindset fiction stories they can read to or with their children. These should echo the themes of growth mindset thinking, such as persistence, the importance of effort and seeing mistakes in a positive light.

- **Talking in terms of effort.** We know that effort is the path to mastery. And that targeted effort is the number one process we want all students to be engaged in. Share these ideas with parents, explain why effort matters so much and then encourage them to talk to their children about effort. You can exemplify this by giving parents a selection of key phrases to use, or by providing a set of exemplar language changes focussed exclusively on effort. Either way, you will be making clear why effort matters and how parents can make the concept a focal point of the conversations they have with their children.

## Three More Parenting Tools

Here are three more parenting tools you can share:

- **Strategy Sharing.** We use strategies to try to solve problems. Encouraging parents to share strategies with their children has a couple of consequences. First, it gives them access to different ways of thinking and different ways of attempting to solve problems. Second, it demonstrates the efficacy of using strategies, switching strategies and trying out new strategies as a means through which to tackle problems. The very act of discussing strategies implies the relevance of thinking about strategies when looking to achieve something. You can encourage parents to share strategies with their children in relation to school work, but so too can you encourage them to share strategies they adopt when trying to solve problems at home or in their working life. Finally, don't forget you can give parents a set of exemplar questions they can use to start conversations with their children about the strategies they've been using at school.

- **Rebranding Mistakes.** We know that mistakes are a good thing, that they present us with opportunities to learn and that when we make them it is usually a sign that the work we are doing is at a suitable level of difficulty. But do parents know this? And do they know the importance of changing children's perception of mistakes, so as to decrease their fear of failure and encourage a more positive attitude toward intellectual risk-taking? Showing parents how to rebrand mistakes means giving them a new way to talk and think about mistakes. It may also mean challenging some of the assumptions parents have about mistakes and failure – assumptions which might have a long history and be deeply held. Still, tackling this is important and, in some cases, can prove liberating for parents.

- **Focussing on Processes.** Our final parenting tool sees us helping parents to focus on the processes their children engage in to produce work. This helps them to switch the focus of discussion from final products to the things which led to those final products being created. The first step is to explain to parents why processes are important. The second step is to give them a set of exemplar questions they can use to engage their children in discussion about processes. The twenty-five process-based questions in Chapter Ten are an excellent starting point. Either share some of these with parents as they are, or adapt them to fit your context.

**Key Points to Take Away**

1) We want students to be hearing growth mindset messages at home, as well as at school.

2) We need to communicate with parents about growth mindsets.

3) Clarity and consistency of communication are key in getting parents on board.

4) Once parents are familiar with growth mindsets, we can give them tools to use at home.

5) Providing examples and models helps to build parental confidence.

# Chapter Ten – Growth Mindset Questions

**Introduction**

Here we have a collection of 175 questions, all designed to help you promote growth mindsets. There are twenty-five questions per chapter (excluding Chapters One and Nine). All the questions are indicative. You can use them as they are, or adapt them to suit your own teaching style and the students with whom you work.

**Getting the Language Right**

1. What if you could do it?
2. What if you just can't do it yet?
3. What do we need to do to be able to do it?
4. How could we work together to change it?
5. What advice would you give to someone who thought they couldn't do it?
6. What makes a good mistake?
7. Can you show me a good mistake?
8. Can you tell me about the best mistake you've made today?
9. How much more have we learned by making mistakes?
10. How would you explain making mistakes to someone who came to our class for the first time?
11. Tell me what you can do. OK, now what do we need to do to go further?
12. What other techniques have you tried?
13. What advice would you give to someone who wanted to give up?
14. What proof do we have that anybody can change their ability?
15. Can you show me how to keep going?
16. If you get stuck, what different strategies can you try?
17. Can you tell me how you'd try to solve a problem you'd never seen before?
18. Can you tell me what makes a growth mindset?
19. What techniques can you use to keep yourself going when things get tough?
20. Why is challenge good?

21. How would you describe determination?
22. What does perseverance look like?
23. Where does effort come from? What does it look like?
24. Can you convince me that effort is a path to mastery?
25. How do you know you're really learning? What does it feel like?

## Changing How Students Perceive Mistakes

1. What was the last good mistake you made?
2. How many good mistakes have we made so far this week?
3. What's the difference between a good mistake and a really good mistake?
4. Why are mistakes the beginning, not the end?
5. How would you explain good mistakes to an alien?
6. Can you show me the different trials you've been through?
7. What did you learn from each of your trials?
8. What name do you prefer – trial and error or trial and improvement? Why?
9. How could you improve it on the next attempt?
10. What did your trial show you? How could you use the information next time?
11. That's an interesting mistake, isn't it?
12. Can you show me the most interesting mistake you've made today?
13. Which of these mistakes do you think is the most interesting? Why?
14. When does a mistake become an interesting mistake? Why?
15. How could we test whether we're likely to make the same mistake again?
16. How do mistakes link to challenge?
17. Is it true that if you're making mistakes then you're having your thinking challenged? Why?
18. What can you learn from failure?
19. Should you give up if you make a mistake? Why?
20. If you keep making the same mistakes, what can you do to improve things?
21. Can you go back through your book and pick out the best mistake you've made so far this year?

22. Are some mistakes better than others? Why?
23. How do mistakes help you to learn?
24. Can you show me how a mistake has helped you to improve your work?
25. What did you learn from each of your attempts?

## Targeting Student Effort

1. What does good effort look like?
2. What's the difference between useful and useless effort?
3. How would you describe effort?
4. Can you show me what really good effort looks like?
5. When did you target your effort most effectively?
6. What strategies did you use to keep going?
7. How do you keep yourself focussed?
8. What advice would you give to someone who felt their effort was waning?
9. Why does effort matter?
10. What are the most important things about effort?
11. Can you give me three reasons why effort matters more than anything else?
12. How does effort help you to learn more?
13. What does it feel like when you're really targeting your efforts?
14. Are there certain things you can do to keep yourself on track? What are they?
15. How can people keep their effort up if they start getting distracted?
16. Can you tell me about a piece of work you did where effort played a really big part?
17. What could we focus on next?
18. How could you use that information to target your effort?
19. If you had to pick one thing to focus your effort on, what would it be?
20. Where does effort come from?
21. What advice would you give to someone who didn't feel like putting in any effort?
22. Can you show me what you've achieved through your own effort?
23. Is there such a thing as bad effort? Why?

24. How would you know if someone had put in a lot of effort?
25. Why is it important to focus your effort?

## Giving Great Feedback

1. Why does feedback matter?
2. What makes feedback important?
3. How can you use feedback to improve your work?
4. What does good feedback sound like?
5. Can you give yourself feedback? Why?
6. What is the best way to use the feedback you get?
7. Is all feedback equally important? Why?
8. Can you show me an example of how you've used feedback to improve your work?
9. Can you tell me what feedback I should give you about this piece of work?
10. Where would feedback be most useful here?
11. Is feedback about you as a person, or about how to get better?
12. Why might it be more useful if I give you feedback on the strategies you've used?
13. Can you show me your best mistake and tell me what feedback it gave you?
14. How could you improve this bit of your work?
15. How could you have done this differently? What might have happened then?
16. If I'd written this, what feedback would you give me? Why?
17. Can you show me how you've improved your work, based on the feedback?
18. Can you talk me through the improvements you've made?
19. How did you decide to use the feedback?
20. How do you plan to use the feedback next time?
21. What could you do if you received feedback you didn't like?
22. So, based on what I've suggested, what could you do next?
23. Who else could give you good feedback on this?
24. Who could you give some good feedback to?
25. Is trial and improvement a way to give yourself feedback? Why?

**Thinking About Thinking**

1. Can you talk me through your thinking?
2. How has your thinking changed?
3. What changed your thinking?
4. How is your thinking different now, compared to the start of the lesson?
5. What are you thinking about while you're doing this?
6. How did you try to solve the problem?
7. What worked? What didn't? Why?
8. How did you think your way through the challenges?
9. What strategies did you use?
10. When you hit the problem, how did you try thinking about it?
11. If you were giving someone advice on how to tackle a problem like this, what would you tell them?
12. What does it feel like when the thinking gets difficult?
13. What if you had to think about it again?
14. How might your thinking change if we went back and tried again?
15. Are there different ways of thinking for different situations?
16. What techniques do you use to help yourself think? How do they work?
17. Is it possible for anybody to change their thinking? Why?
18. Where does thinking come from?
19. What made you change your mind?
20. Is there a better way to think about this? Why?
21. What advice would you give to someone who finds themselves thinking in circles about a problem?
22. How could changing your thinking help you to see the problem differently?
23. How else could we think about this?
24. What questions could someone ask themselves when they are thinking through a problem?
25. What are the best ways to keep your thinking on track? Or is it sometimes good to take it off track...on purpose?

**Creating a Challenge Culture**

1. Can you tell me more about that?
2. Can you tell me again, but this time with more detail?
3. How would you increase the level of challenge here?
4. What would make this task more challenging?
5. If I made this more challenging, how would you respond?
6. What makes something challenging?
7. Why is challenge good?
8. What does challenge look like? What does it feel like?
9. How does challenge help you to learn?
10. How do you know when you are being challenged?
11. What if you had to start again from scratch and do it differently?
12. Why might there be other, better ways to do it?
13. Can you talk me through the bits you found most difficult?
14. What did you do to keep going when it got really tricky?
15. How would you convince someone that challenge is a good thing?
16. If things get tough, what are some of the different ways you can respond?
17. How much challenge is enough?
18. If something doesn't make sense, what then?
19. How could you make this better, even though it looks finished?
20. When were you challenged the most during the lesson? Why?
21. What's the most challenging thing you've done so far this week?
22. What can I do to make the work more challenging for you?
23. If you had to describe challenge as a shape, what would it be?
24. What goes through your mind when you encounter a challenge?
25. What makes challenges good for you?

**Focussing on Processes**

1. What did you do? Talk me through it.
2. How are you thinking about the problem?
3. What ideas do you have for getting started? How might they work in practice?
4. What other strategies could you use? What might be the result?
5. Where did it go wrong? How could we use this information?

6.  If you were going to do it again, how would you change your approach?
7.  What else could you do to get a better end result?
8.  Is there another strategy you could try?
9.  How much better might it be after three more attempts?
10. What did you learn from each attempt? How did you use that to refine your thinking?
11. Why did it end up like this?
12. How could you get a different result through changing what you did?
13. How could you tweak your efforts next time, to get a different result?
14. If you were going to have another go, what changes would you make? Why?
15. Can you explain what someone else would need to go through to get the same result?
16. How does this attempt compare to the last one?
17. How does your thinking now compare to your thinking before?
18. What is the biggest difference between now and then?
19. How are you approaching things differently this time? Why?
20. What makes thinking more effective? Why?
21. How would you describe the thinking you've done?
22. Where did things start to change? What did you do that caused this?
23. If you were going to start again, what would you focus on first?
24. Can you tell me what other options there are? How might these work?
25. What if you had to explain the process to an alien? What would you say?

# Conclusion

So there we have it. More than sixty activities, strategies and techniques you can use to develop growth mindsets in your classroom or school and more than 200 questions you can use to change how students think.

Throughout the book I've tried to demonstrate that developing growth mindsets is a long-term project. It's about changing how students perceive themselves, their learning and what they think is possible. It's about cultivating new habits of mind – and sometimes breaking down old ones.

This doesn't mean that a desire to develop a growth mindset classroom is utopian. Far from it. It just means that change will be gradual and will be partly dependent on you persisting with your mission, even in the face of setbacks.

There will also be moments of surprise and delight along the way. Like when a student starts talking to you, unprompted, about good mistakes. Or when a child who previously thought they were incapable of grasping complex ideas suddenly decides to keep going even when things get challenging.

For these reasons, taking a growth mindsets approach to your teaching is rather unlike most other teaching and learning interventions. It takes you and your class in a different direction, causes you to look at your job from a different perspective. And this is what makes it so powerful. What can lead to major changes in how your students think – maybe even major changes in how you think.

I've included a select bibliography below. This should give you a good start on finding out more about mindsets and further developing your understanding. As I said in the introduction, it is well worth reading both of Carol Dweck's books. They give you a great grounding in the research and provide lots of fascinating examples you can share with your students.

All that's left for me to say is good luck! I hope you've enjoyed reading the book and I hope it helps you to develop growth mindsets in your classroom. I'm sure, with persistence, targeted effort and critical reflection that you'll do a great job.

## Select Bibliography

Mary Cay Ricci – Mindsets in the Classroom: Building a Culture of Success

Angela Duckworth – Grit: The Power of Passion and Perseverance

Charles Duhigg – The Power of Habit

Carol Dweck – Mindset: How You Can Fulfil Your Potential

Carol Dweck – Self-Theories – Their role in Motivation, Personality and Development

Atul Gawande – The Checklist Manifesto

K.A. Ericsson – Development of Professional Expertise

John Hattie – Visible Learning

Barry Hymer and Mike Gershon – The Growth Mindset Pocketbook

Daniel Kahneman – Thinking Fast and Slow

Daniel Levitin – The Organised Mind

Plato – Dialogues

Gordon Stobart – The Expert Learner

Matthew Syed – Black Box Thinking

Matthew Syed – Bounce – The Myth of Talent and the Power of Practice

16838682R00085

Printed in Great Britain
by Amazon